Garden & Outdoor Design

teNeues

Imprint

Editor: Haike Falkenberg

Editorial coordination: Katharina Feuer, Mariel Marohn, Manuela Roth, Text: Haike Falkenberg
Layout: Manuela Roth, Imaging & Pre-press: Janine Minkner
Translations: Connexus GmbH, Sprachentransfer, Berlin

Photo cover (project name): Earthdesigns, © Maria O'Hara (Talking Point)
Photos back cover: Martin Nicholas Kunz (Six Senses Hideaway Hua Hin), Clive Nichols (Charlotte Rowe's Garden, Contemporary Formal Roof Terrace), Jäger & Jäger (Walden)

Photos introduction (page, location): Clive Nichols (page 3, Holland Park/page 14, Contemporary Formal Roof Terrace/page 188, Sundials "Water Wall"), Maria O'Hara (page 4, Talking Point), Jim Fogarty (page 5, Ashburton House with Slat Seat), courtesy Bloom (page 6, Bloom), Geraldine Bruneel (page 7, Elie Saab Residence), Martin Nicholas Kunz (page 8, SALA Phuket Resort & Spa), Amir Schlezinger (page 9, Regent's Park Garden), Nathalie Pasquel (page 10, Beccaria), Peter Clarke, Latitude Group (page 11, South Melbourne Residence), Haike Falkenberg (page 12), Jäger & Jäger (page 13, Walden), Geraldine Bruneel (page 103, Private Desert Retreat)

Produced by fusion publishing GmbH, Berlin   www.fusion-publishing.com

Published by teNeues Publishing Group

teNeues Verlag Gmbh + Co. KG	teNeues Publishing Company	teNeues Publishing UK Ltd.
Am Selder 37	16 West 22nd Street	York Villa, York Road
47906 Kempen, Germany	New York, NY 10010, USA	Byfleet
Tel.: 0049-(0)2152-916-0	Tel.: 001-212-627-9090	KT14 7HX, Great Britain
Fax: 0049-(0)2152-916-111	Fax: 001-212-627-9511	Tel.: 0044-1932-403509
E-mail: books@teneues.de		Fax: 0044-1932-403514

Press department: teNeues France S.A.R.L.
arehn@teneues.de   93, rue Bannier
Tel.: 0049-2152-916-202   45000 Orléans, France
                                                                                      Tel.: 0033-2-38541071
                                                                                      Fax: 0033-2-38625340

www.teneues.com

ISBN: 978-3-8327-9307-4

© 2009 teNeues Verlag GmbH + Co. KG, Kempen

Printed in Italy

Bibliographic information published by the Deutsche Nationalbibliothek.
The Deutsche Nationalbibliothek lists this publication in the Deutsche Nationalbibliografie; detailed bibliographic data are available in the Internet at http://dnb.d-nb.de.

FURNITURE

PRACTICAL AND NECESSARY

DECORATION

Introduction

It is a worldwide phenomenon: the first warm sunbeam of the year lures people outside to the squares and terraces of cafés. Especially for garden and balcony owners amongst us, this is the beginning of the most beautiful time of the year. We enjoy the light under the open sky, the fresh air, the sun, we rejoice in the prospering of the plants—and often this is even more pleasant in good company.

Luckily, landscape architects, designers and manufacturers pour out a cornucopia of ideas and objects over us every year again and again. That way, we can turn our ordinary "garden scene" into a true "garden dream," where style, arrangement and quality do not have to step back behind the comfort and elegance of one's living space. The choice is wider than most people would expect. The following pages present the most innovative ideas that turn the garden or terrace into the new favorite place to be, not only in the first warm days of spring.

Classics are, of course, the various pieces of garden furniture that allow us to sit outside, dine, relax and enjoy weather and nature. Therefore the first chapter of this book is dedicated to them.

However, practical aspects may not be underestimated when it comes to garden design. A lot of inventive ideas for that can be found in chapter two. No matter if you linger to a garden party in an evening gown or carry home a heavy basket of freshly harvested viands—if the ways are paved safely, properly illuminated and are even nice to look at, you can pay full attention to your guests without having to worry.

In the end, chapter three presents a choice of very beautiful decoration ideas for gardens of any size and style.

Haike Falkenberg

Einleitung

Es ist ein weltweit verbreitetes Phänomen: Die ersten warmen Sonnenstrahlen des Jahres locken die Menschen raus auf die Plätze und Terrassen der Cafés. Doch besonders für die Garten- und Balkonbesitzer unter uns beginnt nun die schönste Zeit des Jahres. Wir genießen das Licht unter freiem Himmel, die frische Luft, die Sonne, erfreuen uns am Gedeihen der Pflanzen und oft bereitet uns dies in Gesellschaft noch größeres Vergnügen.

Welch ein Glück, dass Landschaftsarchitekten, Designer und Hersteller jedes Jahr aufs Neue ein wahres Füllhorn von Ideen und Objekten über uns ausschütten. So können wir unseren „Gartenraum" zu einem wahren „Gartentraum" gestalten, in dem Stil, Arrangement und Qualität nicht hinter dem Komfort und der Eleganz der Wohnräume zurückstehen müssen. Die Auswahl ist größer als die meisten Menschen vermuten würden. Die folgenden Seiten präsentieren die innovativsten Ideen, die den eigenen Garten oder die eigene Terrasse nicht nur in den ersten warmen Frühlingstagen zum neuen Lieblingsplatz werden lassen.

Klassiker sind selbstverständlich die verschiedenen Gartenmöbel, die es uns erlauben, draußen zu sitzen, zu speisen, uns auszuruhen, das Wetter und die Natur zu genießen. Ihnen ist daher das erste Kapitel gewidmet.

Praktische Aspekte bei der Gartengestaltung sind jedoch nicht zu unterschätzen. Viele einfallsreiche Ideen dazu finden Sie im zweiten Kapitel. Denn ob Sie nun im Abendkleid zur Gartenparty schlendern oder einen schweren Korb frisch geernteter Köstlichkeiten nach Hause tragen, wenn die Wege sicher angelegt, gut beleuchtet und auch noch hübsch anzusehen sind, können Sie unbesorgt Ihre ganze Aufmerksamkeit den Gästen schenken.

Zu guter Letzt stellt das dritte Kapitel eine Auswahl bildschöner Dekorationsideen für Gärten jeder Größe und jeglichen Stils vor.

Haike Falkenberg

Introduction

Dans le monde entier, le phénomène est largement répandu : dès que les premiers chauds rayons de soleil de l'année se font sentir, les gens affluent sur les places et aux terrasses des cafés. La plus belle partie de l'année commence, plus particulièrement, pour ceux d'entre nous qui possèdent un balcon ou un jardin. Nous profitons de la lumière et du ciel bleu, de l'air frais, du soleil, prenons plaisir à voir pousser les plantes, un plaisir encore accru quand nous le partageons avec d'autres personnes.

A ces moments de bonheur, s'ajoute la véritable corne d'abondance, en idées, en inspirations et en objets de toutes sortes que, chaque année, les paysagistes, les designers et les fabricants préparent à notre intention. C'est ainsi que nous pouvons métamorphoser cet espace extérieur en un véritable « jardin de rêve » dont le style, l'arrangement et la qualité n'ont rien à envier au confort et à l'élégance des intérieurs. Le choix est encore plus étendu que ne le suppose la plupart d'entre nous. Les pages suivantes présentent, à votre intention, les idées les plus innovantes qui feront de votre terrasse ou de votre jardin votre place préférée même après les premières journées chaudes du printemps.

Les différents meubles de jardin constituent, bien entendu, un des classiques de l'aménagement puisqu'ils nous permettent de nous asseoir, de manger et de nous reposer à l'extérieur, en un mot, de jouir du beau temps et de la nature. C'est pourquoi le premier chapitre leur sera réservé.

Toutefois, on saurait sous-estimer les aspects pratiques lors de l'aménagement d'un jardin. Dans le second chapitre, vous trouverez une multitude d'idées à la fois ingénieuses et originales. En effet, que vous flâniez dans une robe de soirée lors d'une fête de jardin, ou que vous portiez un lourd panier débordant des délices que vous venez de récolter, vous pourrez, sans crainte, consacrer votre attention toute entière à vos invités si les chemins sont bien aménagés, bien éclairés et au surplus d'un aspect esthétique.

Pour conclure, le troisième chapitre vous présentera une série de d'idées pour de ravissantes décorations adaptées aux jardins de toutes les grandeurs et de tous les styles.

Haike Falkenberg

Introducción

Es un fenómeno extendido por todo el mundo: cuando aparecen en el año los primeros y cálidos rayos de sol hacen que las personas sientan la llamada que les mueve a salir al exterior y poblar las plazas, los parques y las terrazas de los bares y cafés. En especial para todos los que tenemos un jardín o una terraza, empieza ahora la mejor temporada del año. Cuánto llegamos a disfrutar de la luz bajo el cielo abierto, el aire fresco y el sol y cuánto nos encanta ver los primeros brotes de las plantas y árboles, y si puede ser en compañía, más placer todavía ...

¡Qué suerte que los paisajistas, diseñadores y fabricantes, cada año nos llenan el cuerno de la abundancia con nuevas ideas y objetos para elegir y nos permiten convertir nuestra "habitación jardín" en un "sueño de jardín" con un estilo, unas ideas y una calidad que poco desmerecen ante el confort y la elegancia que ya conseguimos en el interior de la casa! La oferta es mayor de lo que la mayoría de las personas se imaginaría. En las páginas que siguen a continuación le presentamos las ideas más innovadoras para que cuando aparecen los primeros cálidos días de la primavera, pueda convertir su jardín o terraza en su nuevo sitio favorito para estar.

Por supuesto el producto clásico está presentado por los muebles de jardín que nos permiten estar, comer y cenar, incluso descansar fuera y gozar del buen tiempo y de la naturaleza. A todo ello hemos dedicado el primer capítulo.

Los aspectos prácticos que encuentran en la concepción y el diseño del jardín no se tienen que subestimar. Muchas ideas, todas ellas bien pensadas y muy prácticas, las encontrará en el capítulo segundo. Porque cuando usted tiene que pasear por el jardín vestida de fiesta para atender a sus invitados, al igual que cuando salga por el jardín y lleve una pesada cesta llena de frutas frescas es importante que los caminos estén bien hechos, bien iluminados y además que sean bonitos y con ello, cuando las situaciones así lo requieren, poder dedicar su plena atención a los invitados.

Para finalizar, el tercer capítulo presenta una selección de preciosas ideas de decoración de muchos estilos, tanto para los 'pequeños' jardineros como para los 'grandes'.

Haike Falkenberg

Introduzione

È un fenomeno che si osserva in tutto il mondo: i primi caldi raggi del sole attirano gli uomini nelle piazze e sulle terrazze dei caffè. Tuttavia, soprattutto per quelli tra noi che possiedono un giardino o un balcone, comincia il tempo più bello dell'anno. Godiamo all'aperto della luce, dell'aria fresca, del sole, siamo pieni di gioia nell'osservare la crescita delle piante, e spesso tutto questo ci allieta ancora di più se siamo in compagnia.

Quale fortuna che architetti di paesaggi, progettisti e produttori ogni anno riversino su di noi una vera e propria marea di idee e di oggetti. In questo modo possiamo trasformare il nostro "spazio giardino" in un vero e proprio "giardino da sogno", nel quale lo stile, la disposizione e la qualità non sono inferiori al comfort e all'eleganza delle zone abitabili all'interno delle abitazioni. La scelta è più ampia di quanto la maggior parte di noi possa immaginare. Le pagine che seguono presentano le idee più innovative che fanno diventare il nostro giardino o la terrazza il nostro nuovo luogo preferito, e questo non solamente nei primi giorni caldi di primavera.

A questo proposito un classico è rappresentato naturalmente dai diversi mobili da giardino che ci permettono di sederci, di mangiare, di riposarci e di gustare la natura all'aperto. Ad essi è quindi dedicato il primo capitolo.

Non si debbono tuttavia sottovalutare gli aspetti pratici del dare una forma al giardino. Nel secondo capitolo si possono trovare molte idee ingegnose a questo proposito, poiché se desiderate andare a spasso in abito da sera al party che si tiene in giardino, oppure portare a casa una pesante cesta di gustosità appena colte, se i viottoli sono posti in modo sicuro, sono bene illuminati e belli da vedere, potete totalmente dedicarvi ai Vostri ospiti senza preoccupazioni di sorta.

In conclusione, il terzo capitolo presenta una scelta di belle immagini relative a idee di decorazione per giardini di ogni dimensione e di qualsiasi stile.

Haike Falkenberg

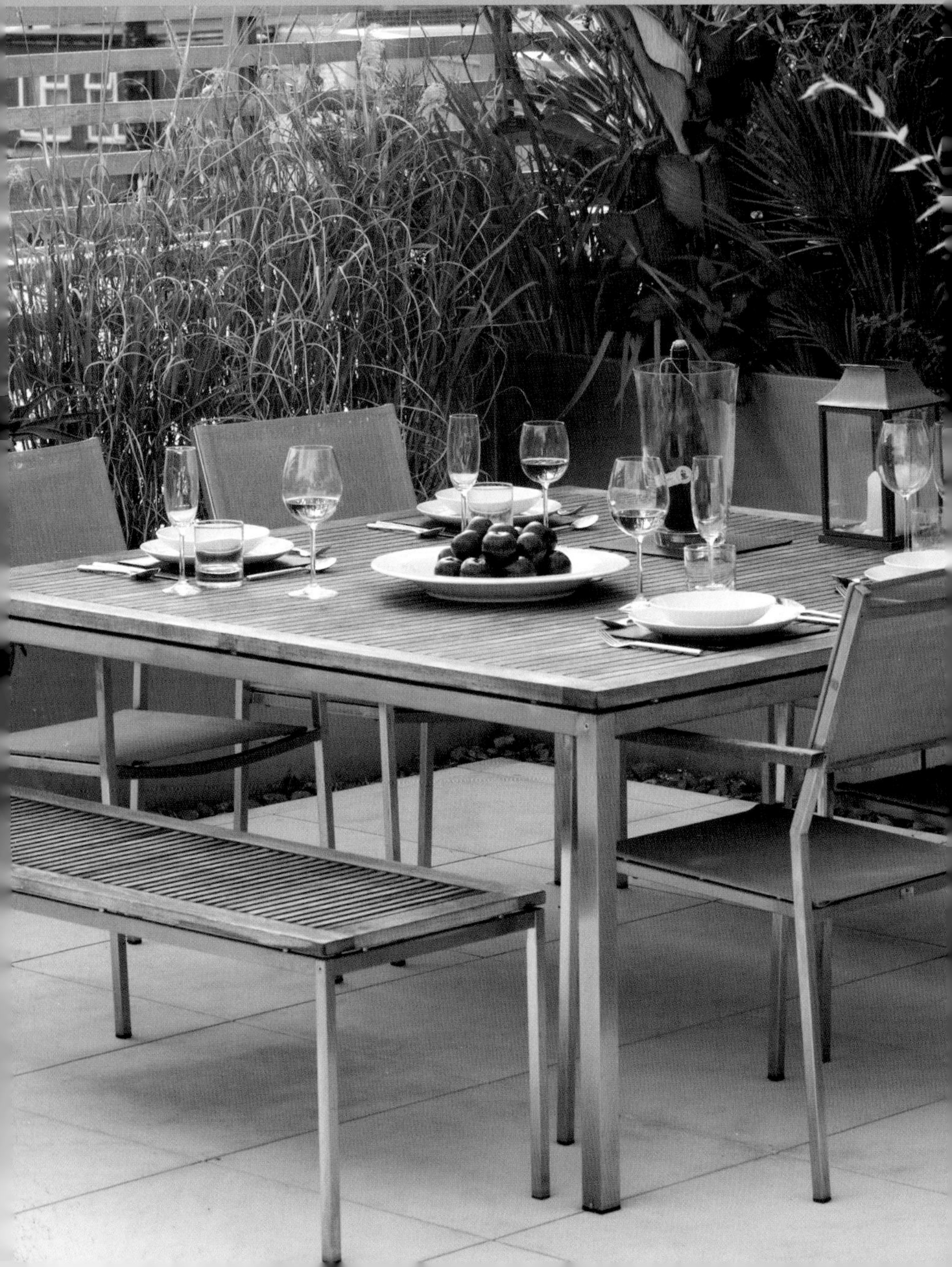

The choice of terrace and garden furniture is as extensive as never before. Functionality, durability, quality and design are in the focus, and classic dining table sets are presented besides sofa corners and all-inclusive solutions like exotic looking lounges or even special customizations. The most commonly used weather-resistant materials are wood, metal, stone, especially developed high-tech artificial fibers or a combination of these materials. Furniture and material adept to the most different garden styles and some designer pieces are even more regarded as objects than as pieces of furniture.

Das Angebot an Terrassen- und Gartenmöbeln ist umfangreich wie nie. Funktionalität, Beständigkeit, Qualität und Design stehen im Vordergrund, klassische Esstischgarnituren stehen neben Sofaecken und Komplettlösungen in Form exotisch anmutender Lounges oder sogar spezieller Maßanfertigungen. Die meist wetterfesten Materialien sind Holz, Metall, Stein, speziell entwickelte High-Tech-Kunstfasern oder eine Kombination dieser Werkstoffe. Möbel und Materialien passen sich den verschiedensten Gartenstilen an, einige Designerstücke sind sogar mehr Objekt als Möbel.

L'offre de meubles de jardin et de terrasse est plus étendue que jamais. La fonctionnalité et la solidité mais aussi le design et la qualité occupent une place de premier plan. Ainsi, on dispose aussi bien d'ensembles « salles à manger » classiques que de coins sofa voire de solutions complètes sous la forme de salons de plein air au charme exotique. On peut souvent obtenir de tels meubles sur mesures. Les matériaux utilisés résistent pour la plupart aux intempéries : le bois, le métal, la pierre, les fibres artificielles high-tech spécialement mises au point ou encore des combinaisons de ces matériaux. Les meubles et les matériaux s'adaptent aux styles de jardin les plus différents, et même, certaines réalisations des designers sont davantage des objets d'art que des meubles.

La oferta de muebles de jardín y terraza es más amplia que nunca. En el enfoque se encuentran la funcionalidad, la resistencia, la calidad y el diseño, y los conjuntos de mesa de comer y sillas más clásicos figuran al lado de rincones de sofás y soluciones completas en forma de Lounges exóticos que invitan a la relajación e incluso fabricaciones especiales a medida. La mayoría de los materiales, todos a prueba de la intemperie, son la madera, los metales, la piedra y fibras sintéticas de alta tecnología desarrolladas expresamente, y también cualquier combinación entre todos ellos que se adapta a los diferentes estilos. También se encuentran piezas menos funcionales que más que muebles nos parecen objetos de diseño.

L'offerta di mobilio per terrazze e giardini non è mai stata così ampia. Funzionalità, resistenza, qualità e design sono le caratteristiche più importanti, ed oltre ai classici accessori per tavole da pranzo si possono ritrovare angoli per sofà e soluzioni complete sotto forma di soggiorni vagamente esotici o perfino di produzioni su misura. I materiali più resistenti alle intemperie sono legno, metallo, pietra, fibre artificiali speciali ad alta tecnologia oppure una combinazione di questi materiali. I mobili ed i materiali si adattano ai più diversi stili di giardino, alcuni elementi di design sono perfino più oggetti astratti che mobili.

Contemporary Formal Roof Terrace

Landscape architecture: Data Nature Associates
Project location: Clerkenwell, London, UK
www.datanature.com
Photos: Clive Nichols

This spacious roof terrace focuses on entertaining; a generous dining table, an outdoor barbecue with bar, designer loungers as well as a sun-screened sitting area next to the hot tub with an inviting view — all constructed using high quality and light materials — increase the internal living area with an additional open-air room.

Diese großzügige Dachterrasse dient vor allem der Gesellligkeit: ein stattlicher Esstisch, ein Open-Air-Barbecue mit Bar, Designerliegen sowie eine sonnengeschützte Sofaecke mit einladendem Ausblick neben dem Whirlpool – alles aus edlen und leichten Materialien – vergrößern den Wohnraum um ein Zimmer unter freiem Himmel.

Cette spacieuse terrasse sur toit se prête surtout à la vie en société : une table de salle à manger imposante, un barbecue et un bar à ciel ouvert, des chaises longues de design ainsi qu'un coin sofa protégé du soleil en proximité d'un whirlpool et des regards engageant – tous les materiaux sont nobles et légers – permettent d'agrandir la surface habitable par une pièce en plein air.

Esta amplísima terraza sobre ático sirve principalmente para socializar; una gran mesa de comer, una barbacoa exterior con bar, tumbonas de diseño así como un rincón de sofas directamente situado al lado de un jacuzzi debidamente protegido contra el sol y con vistas panoramicas – todo realizado en materiales nobles – amplía los metros útiles al añadir una sala de estar debajo el cielo abierto.

Quest'ampia terrazza posta sul tetto è formulata per la vita sociale e l'intrattenimento; un generoso tavolo, un barbecue all'aperto con bar, sdraio d'autore, angolo divani schermati dal sole adiacenti alla vasca idromassaggio e con vista invitante – tutti i materiali sono leggeri e di alta qualità – estendendo lo spazio abitabile interno con una stanza all'aperto.

Modern Lakeside

Landscape architecture and design: AguaFina Gardens International
Project location: Bloomfield Hills, Michigan, USA
Manufacturer: AguaFina Gardens International, www.aguafina.com
Photos: George Dzahristos

This generous garden which frames a state-of-the-art residential house has been designed close to nature. Stone is the predominant material here: antique Asian flagstones pave the ways, light boulders form the lakeshore and even an inventive massive stone table including stools invites to stay.

Der großzügige Garten, der ein modernes Wohnhaus einrahmt, wurde naturnah gestaltet. Stein ist das vorherrschende Material: Antike Steinplatten aus Asien befestigen die Wege, helle Felsblöcke bilden das Seeufer und sogar ein origineller massiver Steintisch samt Hockern lädt zum Verweilen ein.

L'aménagement de ce grand jardin qui entoure une maison d'habitation moderne reste près de la nature. La pierre fournit le matériau dominant : des plaques de pierre d'Asie stabilisent les chemins, des rochers clairs structurent la rive du lac et même une table en pierre massive originale, entourée de tabourets, invite à la flânerie.

El amplio jardín que enmarca la moderna casa unifamiliar se caracteriza por su cercanía a la naturaleza que le envuelve. El material dominante es la piedra: losas antiguas procedentes de Asia fijan los caminos, grandes rocas de color claro forman la orilla del lago e incluso una original mesa de piedra maciza con sus taburetes nos invitan a pasar un rato.

Il generoso giardino che circonda una casa di abitazione moderna viene modellato in modo naturale. La pietra rappresenta il materiale dominante. Antiche piastre di pietra provenienti dall'Asia rafforzano i viottoli, blocchi di pietra chiari costituiscono la riva del lago e perfino una tavola in pietra massiccia completa di sgabelli invita a trattenersi e a contemplare.

Chairs

Design: KOK MAISON
Manufacturer: KOK MAISON
www.kokmaison.com
Photos: courtesy KOK MAISON

Dining Table Color

Design: KOK MAISON
Manufacturer: KOK MAISON
www.kokmaison.com
Photos: courtesy KOK MAISON

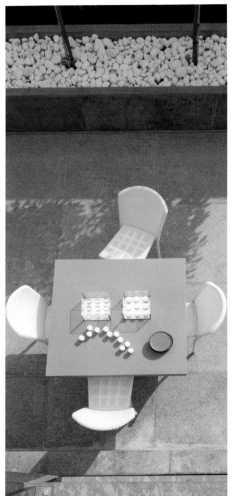

Table Tablabri

Manufacturer: Fermob
www.fermob.com
Photos: courtesy Fermob

Dining Table Na Xemena

Design: Ramon Esteve
Manufacturer: Gandia Blasco
www.gandiablasco.com
Photos: courtesy Gandia Blasco

PicNik

Design: Xavier Lust, Dirk Wynants
Manufacturer: Extremis
www.extremis.be
Photos: Extremis

InUmbra

Design: Dirk Wynants
Manufacturer: Extremis
www.extremis.be
Photos: Extremis

Stream

Design: EOOS
Manufacturer: DEDON
www.dedon.de
Photos: courtesy DEDON

Voido

Design: Ron Arad
Manufacturer: Magis
www.magisdesign.com
Photos: courtesy Magis

MT1

Design: Ron Arad
Manufacturer: Driade
www.driade.com
Photos: courtesy Driade

Clover

Design: Ron Arad
Manufacturer: Driade
www.driade.com
Photos: courtesy Driade

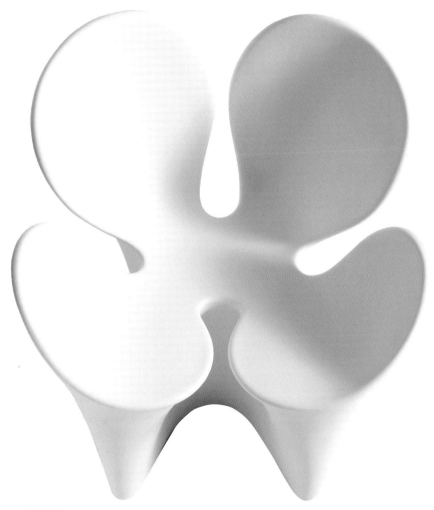

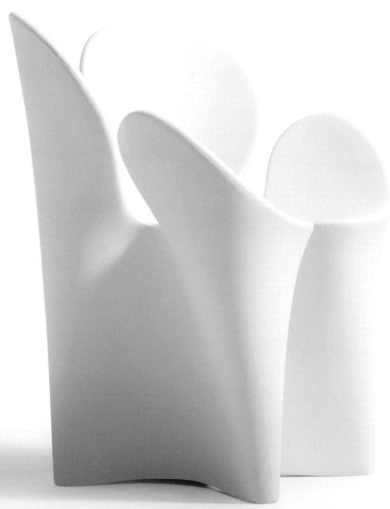

Alias

Manufacturer: Alias
www.aliasdesign.it
Photos: Persani Photo

FURNITURE . Alias   39

Talking Point

Landscape architecture: Katrina Kieffer-Wells, Earth Designs
Project location: Hampstead, London, UK
www.earthdesigns.co.uk
Photos: Maria O'Hara

An L-shaped seating bench with a low table in front and a higher one on the side provides sufficient space for dining with friends. Dark stained sleepers have been used here, which also frame the slightly lowered lounge area—the "Talking Point"—with high poles and shelves.

Eine L-förmige Sitzbank mit einem niedrigen Tisch davor und einem höheren an der Seite bietet ausreichend Raum für ein Essen mit Freunden. Hierfür wurden dunkel gebeizte Bahnschwellen verarbeitet, die auch die leicht abgesenkte Lounge-Zone, den „Talking Point" mit hohen Pfosten und Regalen einrahmen.

Une banquette en L – devant laquelle on trouvera une table basse et une table plus haute sur le côté – offre une place suffisante pour manger avec des amis. Pour cela on a utilisé des traverses de chemin de fer teintées en brun foncé. Celles-ci entourent aussi la zone de salon de plein air un peu en contrebas, le « Talking Point », de poteaux élevés et d'étagères.

Un banco asiento en forma de 'L' con una mesita baja delante y otra más alta en el lado opuesto, ofrecen el espacio más que suficiente para una comida entre amigos. Para conseguirlo, se han utilizado vigas de tren tratadas en oscuro al igual que las que se han dispuesto como altas columnas y estantes, enmarcan la zona de estar ligeramente rebajada que aquí hace de "Talking Point".

Una panchina a forma di L con un tavolo basso davanti ad essa ed uno più alto sul lato offre sufficiente spazio per mangiare con gli amici. A questo scopo sono state lavorate traversine decapate che circondano la zona giorno leggermente abbassata e "l'area di conversazione" caratterizzata da alti pali ed scaffali.

Contemporary Family Garden

Landscape architecture: Chris Maton, Olivebay
Project location: Queens Park, London, UK
www.olivebay.co.uk
Photos: Chris Maton

This lounge is situated in the rear corner of a little city garden and is the perfect place to enjoy the setting sun. The massive wooden bench, which can be indirectly illuminated, becomes cozy thanks to cushions. The bamboo in the back and the wooden espaliers also provide a feeling of security.

Diese Sitzecke befindet sich im hinteren Winkel eines Stadtgärtchens und ist der ideale Platz, um die Abendsonne zu genießen. Die massive Holzbank, die indirekt beleuchtet werden kann, wird durch Kissen gemütlich. Der Bambus im Rücken und Holzspaliere an den Seiten sorgen ebenfalls für Geborgenheit.

Ce banc d'angle se trouve dans le coin arrière d'un petit jardin de ville et représente l'endroit idéal pour profiter du soleil des fins d'après-midi. Des coussins accentuent la convivialité de ce banc en bois massif pourvu d'un éclairage indirect. Des bambous à l'arrière et des espaliers de bois sur le côté renforcent encore l'atmosphère intime de ce lieu.

El sitio para sentarse se encuentra en el rincón más alejado de este jardín público y es el lugar más adecuado para gozar del agradable sol de la tarde. El banco de madera maciza que puede ser iluminado indirectamente, se convierte en confortable por el cojín, mientras que el bambú de la parte trasera y el emparrado lateral de madera vienen a subrayar la sensación de seguridad.

Questo angolo soggiorno si trova nell'angolo posteriore di un piccolo giardino cittadino e rappresenta il luogo ideale per godere del sole che tramonta. La panchina in legno massiccio, che può essere illuminata indirettamente, diventa comoda grazie all'utilizzo di cuscini. Anche il bambù posto sulla parte posteriore e le spalliere in legno sui lati aiutano a creare una sensazione di sicurezza.

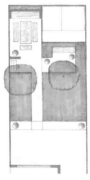

Holland Park

Landscape architecture: Charlotte Sanderson Garden & Landscape Design
Project location: Holland Park, London, UK
Photos: Clive Nichols

DEDON's large lounge strikes the eye on the three terraces of resistant Portland lime stone. Two black Paolo Lenti sunloungers can be found a little elevated on the one side, and a gas-powered grill on the other side. The wooden table is perfect for beautiful dinners in the family circle.

Auf den drei Terrassen aus widerstandsfähigem Portland-Kalkstein fällt die weitläufige Sitzgruppe der Firma DEDON ins Auge. Ein wenig erhöht stehen auf der einen Seite zwei schwarze Sonnenliegen von Paolo Lenti, auf der anderen Seite ein gasbetriebener Grill. Im Familienkreis kann am hölzernen Esstisch gespeist werden.

Sur les trois terrasses en pierres à chaux de Portland résistantes, le vaste groupe de fauteuils de la maison DEDON capte les regards. Un peu au-dessus, se trouve, d'un côté, deux chaises longues noires de Paolo Lenti et, de l'autre côté, un grill au gaz. En toute intimité, la famille peut ainsi prendre un repas sur une table de bois.

En las tres terrazas de mortero Portland de cal y arena, lo que destaca es el amplio grupo para descansar de la firma DEDON. En un plano ligeramente más elevado se encuentran dos tumbonas de color negro del diseñador Paolo Lenti, el lado contrario lo ocupa un grill activado por gas. Reunida la familia entre sí, para las comidas se prepara la mesa de madera.

Sulle tre terrazze in pietra calcarea Portland resistente si nota lo spazioso gruppo tavoli della ditta DEDON. In posizione un poco più elevata, su un lato si trovano due sedie a sdraio di Paolo Lenti, sull'altro lato una griglia a gas. Insieme ai famigliari si può mangiare sulla tavola in legno.

Ashburton House with Slat Seat

Landscape architecture: Jim Fogarty Design Pty Ltd/Jo Philippsohn Simhi of dwell by jo
Project location: Melbourne, Australia
www.jimfogartydesign.com.au, www.dwellbyjo.com.au
Photos: courtesy dwell by jo, Jim Fogarty

Jim Fogarty smartly uses different colored paving stones and wood to give this little garden a diversified structure without sealing too much of the surface. The individual benches made of New Guinea Rosewood and stainless steel, named "Slat" of dwell by jo, appear like art objects on the slightly elevated terrace.

Jim Fogarty setzt geschickt verschiedenfarbige Pflastersteine und Holz ein, um diesen kleinen Garten abwechslungsreich zu strukturieren, ohne zu viel Fläche zu versiegeln. Die individuellen Bänke aus „New Guinea Rosewood" und Edelstahl, „Slat" von dwell by jo, muten auf der leicht erhöhten Terrasse wie Kunstobjekte an.

Pour varier les formes et les structures de ce petit jardin sans pour autant sceller le sol Jim Fogarty a savamment combiné des pavés de pierre et de bois. Les bancs individualisés en « New Guinea Rosewood » et en acier spécial « Slat » de dwell by jo sont mis en relief comme des objets d'art sur cette terrasse légèrement surélevée.

Para evitar de antemano toda monotonía y con la habilidad que le caracteriza, Jim Fogarty utilizó adoquines de distinto color y madera para estructurar este pequeño jardín sin sellar demasiado la superficie disponible. Los bancos aislados fabricados en madera de "New Guinea Rosewood" y el acero inoxidable "Slat" de dwell by jo, a primera vista parecen objetos de arte tal y como se han ubicado en la terraza ligeramente más elevada.

Jim Fogarty inserisce con abilità pietre da pavimentazione stradale di diversi colori e legno, al fine di strutturare questo piccolo giardino in modo vario, senza sigillare troppa superficie. Sulla terrazza leggermente elevata le singole panche "Slat" in legno di "New Guinea Rosewood" e in acciaio inox di dwell by jo hanno l'aspetto di oggetti d'arte.

FURNITURE . Ashburton House with Slat Seat

HOUSE H

Architecture: YES-ARCHiTECTURE
Project location: Steiermark, Austria
www.yes-architecture.com
Photos: FOTO CROCE

Slim Line

Design: Jean-Marie Massaud
Manufacturer: DEDON
www.dedon.de
Photos: courtesy DEDON

Chair Palazzo

Design: La Hutte Design
Manufacturer: La Hutte
www.lahutte-mobilier.com
Photos: courtesy La Hutte

A Tribute to Linnaeus

Landscape architecture: Ulf Nordfjell
Construction company: Brambles Hertfordshire
Photos: Clive Nichols

Blofield

Design: Jeroen van de Kant
Manufacturer: Blofield B.V.
www.blofield.com
Photos: Blofield

Bubble Rock Canape

Design: Living Divani
Manufacturer: Living Divani
www.livingdivani.it
Photos: courtesy Living Divani

Canasta

Design: Patricia Urquiola
Manufacturer: B&B Italia
www.bebitalia.it
Photos: Fabrizio Bergamo

Néo Livingstones

Landscape architecture: Jean Jacques Lecuru
Furniture design and manufacturer: smarin
www.lecuru.com, www.smarin.net
Photos: smarin

Egg

Design: Jørgen Ditzel Nanna
Manufacturer: BONACINA PIERANTONIO SRL
www.bonacinapierantonio.it
Photos: courtesy BONACINA PIERANTONIO

Na Xemena

Design: Ramon Esteve
Manufacturer: Gandia Blasco
www.gandiablasco.com
Photos: courtesy Gandia Blasco

Garden Bench

Design: David Trubridge Ltd.
Manufacturer: David Trubridge Ltd.
www.davidtrubridge.com
Photos: David Trubridge

Stone Lounger

Design: AguaFina Gardens International
Manufacturer: AguaFina Gardens International
www.aguafina.com
Photos: George Dzahristos

Deck Chairs in Singita Sweni Lodge

Project location: Kruger National Park, South Africa
www.singita.com
Photos: Roland Bauer

Summer Cloud

Design: EOOS
Manufacturer: DEDON
www.dedon.de
Photos: courtesy DEDON

Outdoor Rocking Recliner

Design: David Trubridge
Manufacturer: David Trubridge Ltd.
www.davidtrubridge.com
Photos: David Trubridge

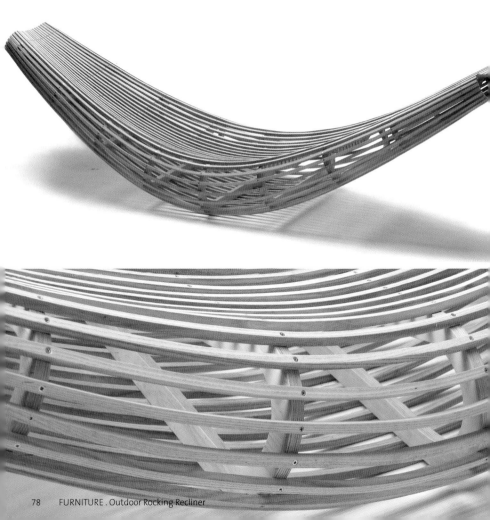

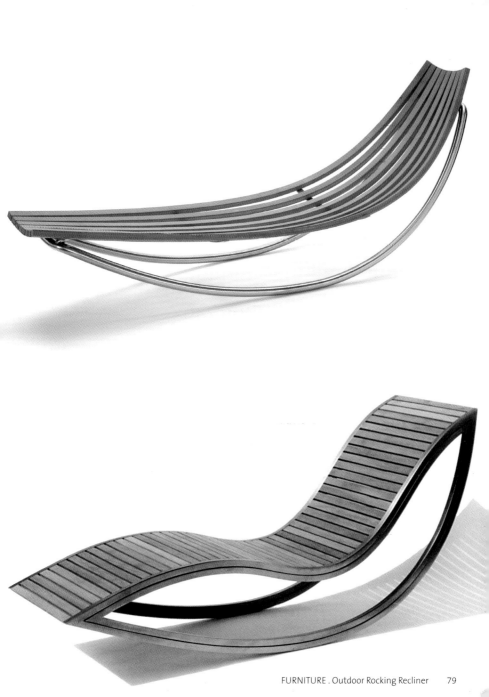

Lounger Atlantic

Design: La Hutte Design
Manufacturer: La Hutte
www.lahutte-mobilier.com
Photos: courtesy La Hutte

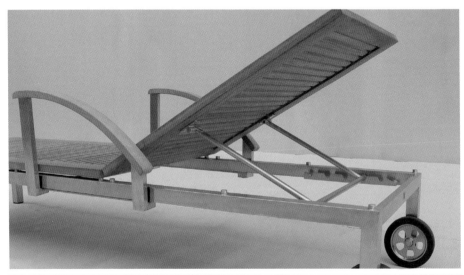

Springtime

Design: Jean-Marie Massaud
Manufacturer: B&B Italia
www.bebitalia.it
Photos: Fabrizio Bergamo

Gandia Blasco

Manufacturer: Gandia Blasco
www.gandiablasco.com
Photos: courtesy Gandia Blasco

Exonido – A Room to Live Outdoors

Design: Christophe Schmitt
Manufacturer: Exonido
www.exonido.fr
Photos: Christophe Schmitt

The concept from "Exonido", which has been distinguished at the Design Biennale of St. Étienne in France in 2008, combines precious materials that fulfill the standards of a sustainable development to end up in a likeable overall solution that provides protection from insights, sun and wind. Multiple design varieties and accessories can be chosen for this design.

Das 2008 auf der Design Biennale von St. Étienne in Frankreich hervorgehobene Konzept von „Exonido" vereint noble Materialien, welche die Standards nachhaltiger Entwicklung erfüllen, zu einer sympathischen Komplettlösung, die Sicht-, Sonnen- und Windschutz bietet. Mehrere Designvarianten und Accessoires stehen zur Wahl.

La conception d'Exonido a été distingué à l'occasion de la Biennale du design de Saint-Étienne en France. Elle allie des matériaux nobles qui répondent aux exigences du développement durable. Elle constitue une solution complète qui offre, à la fois, une protection contre le vent, le soleil et les regards indiscrets. On dispose de plusieurs variantes concernant le design et les accessoires.

El concepto de "Exonido" destacado en la feria bianual de diseño de 2008 en la ciudad francesa de St. Étienne, combina el uso de materiales nobles que cumplen los estándares del desarrollo sostenible, en una solución global simpática que ofrece protección tanto de la vista indiscreta, como del sol y del viento. Incluso se puede decidir entre distintas variantes de diseño y de accesorios.

Il concetto di "Exonido" premiato nel 2008 alla Design Biennale di St. Étienne in Francia unisce materiali nobili, che rispettano gli standard di sviluppo sostenibile, facendolo diventare una simpatica soluzione completa che offre protezione dallo sguardo di estranei, dal sole e dal vento. Sono disponibili diverse varianti di design e di accessori.

Avant ou après ?

Kingdom Gazebo

Design: Honeymoon
Manufacturer: Honeymoon World
www.honeymoon-world.com
Photos: Gregory Dubrulle

There is enough space for even a whole garden parlor under the wide projecting thatched roof of the "Kingdom" design. The solid structure of sustainably cultivated teak wood and the detachable cushion covers made of high-quality Sunbrella material leave nothing to be desired in terms of elegance, comfort and quality.

Unter dem weit ausladenden Strohdach des Modells „Kingdom" findet ein kompletter Salon für den Garten Platz. Die stabile Struktur aus nachhaltig bewirtschaftetem Teakholz sowie die abnehmbaren Kissenbezüge aus hochwertigem Sunbrella-Stoff lassen in Bezug auf Eleganz, Komfort und Qualität keine Wünsche offen.

Un salon de jardin complet trouve sa place sous le vaste toit en chaume du modèle « Kingdom ». Sa structure robuste est en Teck massif – un bois qui répond aux critères de développement durable – et le salon est notamment équipé avec des housses amovibles en tissus Sunbrella haut de gamme, tout cela pour un résultat qui allie élégance, confort et qualité.

Debajo del tejado de paja y el enorme vuelo que caracteriza al modelo "Kingdom" cabe una sala de estar completa para el jardín. La estructura estable de madera de teca tratada para larga duración, al igual que las fundas de cojín fabricadas con la valiosa tela Sunbrella y desmontables en su totalidad, parece que tienen cubiertos todos los requisitos en lo que hace referencia a la elegancia, el confort y la calidad.

Sotto il tetto di paglia molto sporgente del modello "Kingdom" si trova un salone completo per il giardino. La struttura stabile in legno di tek, che rispetta gli standard di gestione sostenibile, nonché i rivestimenti asportabili per cuscini in tessuto Sunbrella di notevole valore, non lasciano a desiderare quanto ad eleganza, comfort e qualità.

Sunrise Gazebo

Design: Honeymoon
Manufacturer: Honeymoon World
www.honeymoon-world.com
Photos: Michel Coste

Slightly elevated and accessible over three stairs, the "Sunrise" lounge is an enchanting place to sit for six to eight persons which sophisticatedly combines uncongested comfort and protection from sun or rainfall. The lounge can be turned into a dining place in the twinkling of an eye.

Leicht erhöht und über drei Stufen zugänglich ist die Lounge „Sunrise" ein zauberhafter Sitzplatz für sechs bis acht Personen, der luftige Behaglichkeit und Schutz vor Sonne oder Niederschlägen auf anspruchsvollste Weise vereint. Die Lounge kann im Handumdrehen in einen Essplatz verwandelt werden.

Le salon « Sunrise » est légèrement surélevé et on y accède par trois marches. Il offre une assise confortable pour un groupe de six à huit personnes qui désire profiter de moments agréables, à l'abri du soleil ou de la pluie, dans une ambiance satisfaisant aux plus hautes exigences. En un tour de main, ce salon de plein air peut se transformer en salle à manger.

En un plano ligeramente más elevado, accesible franqueando tres peldaños, el Lounge "Sunrise" ofrece un rincón de ensueño para que se puedan sentar de seis a ocho personas, en medio de la agradable brisa que viene del mar y a la vez protegidas contra el sol y los chaparrones repentinos, en un ambiente de todo confort. Todo el Lounge se puede convertir en una mesa para comer en un abrir y cerrar de ojos.

Leggermente sopraelevato ed accessibile attraverso tre gradini è il soggiorno "Sunrise", un incantevole posto a sedere per sei a otto persone, il quale unisce in modo esigente una comodità ventilata e la protezione da raggi del sole o da precipitazioni. Il soggiorno può essere trasformato in un istante in un posto tavola.

Honeymoon Daybed

Design: Honeymoon
Manufacturer: Honeymoon World
www.honeymoon-world.com
Photos: Michel Coste

Walden

Design: Nils Holger Moormann GmbH
Manufacturer: Nils Holger Moormann GmbH
www.moormann.de
Photos: Jäger & Jäger

This beautifully grained larch wood object has a lot to offer. It can be placed in almost any location and has a whole set of garden equipment down pat in no time at all: from utensils to a garden hose and a roofed seat, culminating in a swivel-out barbecue place.

Dieses Objekt aus hübsch gemasertem Lärchenholz hat es in sich. Man kann es beinahe an jedem beliebigen Ort aufstellen und hat im Handumdrehen eine komplette Gartenausstattung parat: von Arbeitsutensilien über einen Gartenschlauch und einen überdachten Sitzplatz bis hin zum aus-schwenkbaren Grill.

Cette objet en bois de mélèze aux belles veinures ne manque pas de produire le meilleur effet. On peut la placer où l'on veut et l'on dispose en un tour de main d'un équipement de jardin complet : des ustensiles de travail ainsi que d'un tuyau d'arrosage, d'une place assise couverte de même que d'un grill pivotant.

Este objeto fabricado en madera de alerce con sus preciosas vetas da mucho de sí. Se puede colocar prácticamente en cualquier lugar para disponer de manera rápida de un equipamiento para jardín casi completo: desde los utensilios de trabajo, pasando por una manguera de jardín y un asiento cubierto, así como un grill desplegable.

Questo obietto in larice elegantemente venata ha molto in sé. La si può mettere quasi in qualsiasi luogo, ed in questo modo in un istante si ha pronta una dotazione per giardino completa: utensili di lavoro, un tubo d'irrigazione ed un posto a sedere coperto ed una griglia ripiegabile.

The investment into the appropriate material for a terrace that is tailored exactly to one's estate, the installation of paths and the construction of a screen or wind protection always pays off in the long run. Precious materials, successful combinations and attractive designs let your garden look good even in bad weather conditions and guarantee for safety and user-friendliness at the same time. And in good weather conditions, the garden's possibilities of use multiply thanks to these cleverly designed areas.

Die Investition in das passende Material für eine auf das Grundstück zugeschnittene Terrasse, die Anlage von Wegen oder das Errichten eines Sicht- und Windschutzes zahlt sich auf lange Sicht immer aus. Edle Materialien, gelungene Kombinationen und ansprechende Muster lassen den Garten sogar bei schlechtem Wetter gut aussehen, und gewährleisten gleichzeitig Sicherheit und Benutzerfreund-lichkeit. Und bei schönem Wetter vervielfältigen sich durch diese durchdacht gestalteten Bereiche die Nutzungsmöglichkeiten des Gartens.

A long terme, les investissements nécessaires pour les matériaux s'avèrent toujours rentables, qu'il s'agisse de l'aménagement d'une terrasse spécialement conçue en fonction du terrain disponible, du tracé de chemins ou de protections contre le vent et les regards indiscrets. Des matériaux nobles, des combinaisons réussies et des formes appropriées confèrent au jardin un cachet esthétique qui demeure même lorsque le temps est mauvais. De plus, ils sécurisent cet espace et en facilitent l'utilisation. Lorsque le temps est agréable, ces aménagements mûrement réfléchis multiplient encore les possibilités d'utilisation du jardin.

A medio y largo plazo, las inversiones realizadas con el material adecuado para un jardín perfecta-mente adaptado al terreno, la creación de caminos o la colocación de una verja de protección para brindarnos privacidad y protección contra el viento, siempre se rentabilizan. El uso de materiales no-bles, combinaciones acertadas y un diseño adecuado, hacen que el jardín tenga un aspecto aceptable incluso cuando el tiempo no invita, a la vez que ofrecen seguridad y facilidad en el mantenimiento. Cuando el tiempo es bueno los esfuerzos dedicados a la realización de las distintas zonas multiplican las posibilidades de uso del jardín en su conjunto.

L'investimento nel materiale adatto per una terrazza realizzata su un appezzamento, per il quale col tempo vale sempre la pena realizzare un sistema di viottoli o erigere una protezione per la vista o il vento. Materiali nobili, combinazioni riuscite e modelli adatti danno al giardino un ottimo aspetto anche in caso di cattivo tempo, e assicurano allo stesso tempo sicurezza e facilità d'uso. E in caso di bel tempo, grazie a queste aree realizzate appositamente si moltiplicano le possibilità di utilizzo del giardino.

Derbez Garden I

Landscape architecture: Derbez Paysage (Bureau d'etude)
Project location: St. Tropez, France
www.derbez-paysage.com
Photos: Patrick Berlan, www.patrickberlan-studio.com

The scope for natural stone designs is almost unlimited. Support walls, stairs and a small amphitheater have been built of colored lime sandstone in this South French garden, while large, randomly shaped flags pave ways through the lawn or frame beds in a majestic way.

Die Gestaltungsmöglichkeiten mit Naturstein sind nahezu grenzenlos. In diesem südfranzösischen Garten wurden Stützmauern, Treppen und ein kleines Amphitheater aus buntem Kalksandstein errichtet, während große, willkürlich geformte Platten Wege durch den Rasen ziehen oder majestätisch ein Beet einfassen.

Les pierres naturelles offrent des répertoires de formes et de structures presque illimités. Des murs de soutien mais aussi des escaliers et même un petit amphithéâtre en grès calcaire coloré ont été érigés dans ce jardin du sud de la France. En même temps, de grandes plaques aux formes arbitraires créent des chemins à travers le gazon ou entourent des parterres, majestueusement.

Las posibilidades de diseño que ofrece la piedra natural, prácticamente no tiene límites. En este jardín en el Sur de Francia se construyeron con piedras areniscas multicolores, tanto los muros de contención y las escaleras, como un anfiteatro, a la vez que grandes placas del mismo material de formas debidas al azar están trazando sendas a través del césped o bien, de manera majestuosa, delimitan una zona de flores.

Le possibilità di allestimento con pietra naturale sono pressoché infinite. In questo giardino della Francia meridionale, murature di sostegno, scale e un piccolo anfiteatro sono stati eretti in pietra arenaria calcarea, mentre grandi viottoli realizzati in lastre di varie forme sono state tracciate nell'erba o circondano maestosamente un'aiuola.

Moreira

Landscape architecture: Slomp & Busarello Architects
Project location: Curitiba, Brazil
www.slompbusarello.com.br
Photos: Slomp & Busarello

Fancy natural stone walls frame some of the beds as well as mainly the sides of the long outside stairway. Slender flagstones have therefore been artfully piled up so that the latter form an enchanting scenery for the plants with their cream white to reddish and brownish beige fickle colors.

Aparte Mauern aus Naturstein fassen einige der Beete sowie vor allem die Seiten der langen Außentreppe ein. Dazu wurden schmale Steinplatten kunstvoll aufgeschichtet, so dass die von Cremeweiß bis zu rötlichem und bräunlichem Beige changierenden Farbtöne eine zauberhafte Kulisse für die Pflanzen bilden.

Des murs élégants en pierres naturelles enchâssent quelques-uns des parterres, en particulier ceux qui se trouvent sur les côtés du long escalier extérieur. A cet effet, de minces plaques de pierre ont été empilées avec art de sorte qu'elles constituent, vis à vis des plantes, une coulisse aux tons changeant : du crème aux beiges rougeâtres et marron.

Bonitos muros realizados en piedra natural sirven para enmarcar algunos de los bancales y, sobre todo, los lados de la larga escalera exterior. Para conseguirlo se han apilado de forma muy artesana centenares de placas de piedra estrechas y se ha hecho de tal forma que las tonalidades de color cambiantes, desde el blanco crema pasando por los beiges rojizos hasta marrones, llegando a formar un decorado precioso y único para las plantas.

Graziose murature in pietra naturale cingono alcune delle aiuole nonché soprattutto i lati della lunga scala esterna. A questo scopo, strette lastre di pietra sono state abilmente disposte a strati, così che le tonalità di colore che mutano, passando dal bianco crema al beige rossastro e tendente al marrone, costituiscono un magico sfondo per le piante.

PRACTICAL AND NECESSARY . Moreira

Derbez Garden II

Landscape architecture: Derbez Paysage (Bureau d'etude)
Project location: Ramatuelle, France
www.derbez-paysage.com
Photos: Patrick Berlan, www.patrickberlan-studio.com

Gardens located on a slope are always a challenge. Various light stone support walls draw geometric patterns into the landscape in this Mediterranean Sea garden. The choice of small stones and the accentuation of verticals by different trees take some strictness from this ensemble.

Gärten in Hanglage stellen immer eine Herausforderung dar. In diesem Mittelmeergarten zeichnen vielfältige Stützmauern aus hellem Naturstein geometrische Muster in die Landschaft. Die Wahl kleiner Steine und die Betonung der Vertikalen durch verschiedene Bäume nimmt dem Ensemble die Strenge.

Les jardins aménagés sur une pente constituent toujours un défi particulier. Dans ce jardin méditerranéen, des murs de soutien variés en pierres naturelles claires dessinent des formes géométriques dans le paysage. Grâce au choix de petites pierres et à l'accentuation des lignes verticales par différents arbres, la sévérité de l'ensemble est atténuée.

Tener y mantener un buen jardín situado en una colina supone siempre un reto especial. Este jardín mediterráneo se caracteriza por sus muros de contención de piedra natural clara que parecen dibujar figuras geométricas en el paisaje de su entorno. La elección de las piedras pequeñas y el énfasis que se concede a las líneas verticales mediante el uso de distintos árboles, ayuda a quitar un poco el rigor que el conjunto parece irradiar.

I giardini posti su un pendio rappresentano sempre una sfida. In questo giardino mediterraneo molteplici murature di protezione in pietra naturale chiara disegnano modelli geometrici nel panorama. La scelta di pietre di piccole dimensioni e l'accentuazione della verticalità per mezzo di alberi di diverso tipo toglie forza all'insieme.

SALA Phuket Resort & Spa

Landscape architecture: Department of Architecture
Project location: Phuket, Thailand
www.salaphuket.com
Photos: Martin Nicholas Kunz

Two colors are defining the picture here: light green and strong grey. The fact that this easy-care and practical strip design does not have a rigid effect for terraces and paths in the tropical climate, is thanks to the design being interrupted by small grassy rectangles and alternating mown and unmown areas.

Zwei Farben bestimmen das Bild: helles Grün und kräftiges Grau. Dass die im tropischen Klima pflegeleichte und praktische Streifenlösung für Terrassen und Wege nicht starr wirkt, liegt an der Unterbrechung des Musters durch kleine grasbewachsene Rechtecke sowie der Abwechslung gemähter und ungemähter Flächen.

Deux couleurs déterminent l'impression générale : un vert clair et un gris soutenu. Les bandes – d'un entretien aisé et pratiques sous un climat tropical – n'ont pas ici un effet trop rigide comme solution employée pour les terrasses et les chemins. Cela tient à ce que ce schéma est interrompu par de petits carrés d'herbe et par l'alternance de surfaces de gazon coupées et non coupées.

Son dos los colores que claramente dominan el cuadro: el verde pálido y el gris fuerte. El hecho de que la solución de rayas para las terrazas y los caminos, que aquí en el clima tropical, carece de su habitual efecto de rigidez, se debe a la interrupción del diseño por los pequeños rectángulos de césped, así como la alternancia de las superficies cortadas y sin cortar.

Due colori costituiscono questa figura: verde chiaro e grigio forte. Il motivo per il quale nel clima dei tropici una soluzione a strisce di facile manutenzione e pratica per terrazze e viottoli non dà un'impressione di staticità è dovuto alla rottura del modello attraverso rettangoli erbosi e grazie alla varietà rappresentata da superfici tagliate e non.

Garden Paths

Landscape architecture: Derbez Paysage (pages 118–121)
www.derbez-paysage.com
Photos: Patrick Berlan (pages 118–121), Clive Nichols (pages 122, 123)

Six Senses Hideaway Hua Hin

Landscape architecture: Eva Malmstrom
Project location: Hua Hin, Thailand
www.sixsenses.com
Photos: Martin Nicholas Kunz

A play of different levels seems to connect heaven and earth. Lower protected lounges position the viewer's eye on the water level of the pools and ponds, so that the light stone terraces appear like footbridges.

Ein Spiel verschiedener Ebenen scheint Himmel und Erde miteinander zu verbinden. Tiefer liegende geschützte Sitzecken positionieren den Blick des Betrachters auf Höhe des Wasserspiegels der Pools und Becken, so dass die hellen Steinterrassen wie Stege erscheinen.

Un jeu réunissant différents niveaux donne ici l'impression de relier le ciel et la terre. Des groupes de sièges protégés situés en contrebas dirige le regard au niveau de la surface de l'eau des piscines et des bassins si bien que les terrasses en pierres claires semblent être des quais.

El juego con los distintos niveles y planos parece unir el cielo con la tierra. Rincones para sentarse protegidos en un plano más bajo, posicionan la vista del observador a la altura del nivel de agua de las piscinas y estanques, de modo que las terrazas de piedra clara aparentan ser embarcaderos.

Un gioco di diversi livelli sembra di unire tra loro cielo e terra. Angoli soggiorno più in basso posizionano l'occhio dell'osservatore all'altezza dello specchio d'acqua delle piscine e delle vasche, così che le chiare terrazze in pietra appaiono come passerelle.

Grosvenor Waterside

Landscape architecture: Amir Schlezinger
Project location: South West London, UK
www.mylandscapes.co.uk
Photos: Amir Schlezinger

The high-quality material range and the excellent processing make the attraction of this roof terrace. Large sandstone flags diagonally meet a deck of Balau wood. The grey powder coating of the tailored planters underlines the warm shade of the wood, which has also been used to build a bench and a screen.

Die hochwertige Materialpalette sowie die exzellente Verarbeitung machen den Reiz dieser Dachterrasse aus. Große Sandsteinplatten stoßen diagonal an ein Deck aus Balau-Holz. Die graue Puderbeschichtung der maßgefertigten Pflanzkübel unterstreicht den warmen Ton des Holzes, aus dem auch eine Bank und ein Sichtschutz gebaut wurden.

La gamme des matériaux nobles ainsi que l'excellence du traitement de ces matériaux constituent l'attrait de ce toit-terrase. De grandes plaques de grès coupent à la diagonale un niveau de bois de balau. Le revêtement par poudre gris des cubes pour plantes met en relief les tons chauds du bois utilisé aussi pour la confection d'un banc ainsi que d'un paravent.

La amplia paleta de materiales nobles en combinación con la elaboración perfecta de todos los detalles confiere un particular encanto a este ático. Grandes placas de piedras areniscas chocan diagonalmente con una cubierta realizada en madera Balau. El recubrimiento de polvo de color gris que presentan las macetas hechas a medida, viene a subrayar el tono suave de la madera con la que también se ha fabricado un banco y un tapa vistas.

l'offerta di materiale di pregio nonché l'eccellente lavorazione rappresentano l'elemento di attrazione di questa terrazza su tetto. Grandi piastre in pietra arenaria si scontrano diagonalmente con tetto in legno balau. Il grigio rivestimento, posto quasi come cipria, dei vasi per piante realizzati a misura sottolinea il tono caldo del legno, con il quale è stata costruita anche una panchina e una staccionata.

Contemporary Architectural Garden

Landscape architecture: Charlotte Rowe Garden Design
Project location: Kensington, London, UK
www.charlotterowe.com
Photos: Clive Nichols, Light IQ

These two linked terraces are, at the same time, modern and welcoming. The pale cream Portuguese lime stone paving perfectly complements the brick boundary walls of the garden and timber of the trellis and planters. A key feature is the planted 'rill' which, like the small water feature, is filled with polished black pebbles.

Modern und freundlich sind diese beiden klar voneinander getrennten Terrassen. Der portugiesische Kalkstein harmoniert mit dem Klinker der Seitenmauern sowie dem Holz der Spaliere und Pflanzcontainer. Markanter Blickfang ist die bepflanzte Rinne, die wie das kleine Wasserbecken mit schwarzen Kieseln ausgelegt ist.

Ces deux terrasses clairement séparées l'une de l'autre sont tout à la fois modernes et accueillantes. Le calcaire portugais s'harmonise aux briques des murs latéraux ainsi qu'au bois des espaliers et des conteneurs. Le point de mire de l'ensemble est constitué par une bande centrale ou le vert de la végétation est bordé par des galets noirs identiques à ceux du petit bassin.

Estas dos terrazas claramente separadas la una de la otra se caracterizan ambas por su aspecto moderno y alegre. La piedra arenisca portuguesa armoniza perfectamente con la piedra vista de los muros laterales, al igual que lo hace con la madera de las celosías y el macetón para flores. Lo cautivador de las vistas es el canalón con plantas cuyo fondo, al igual que el pequeño estanque de agua, se encuentra cubierto de cantos rodados negros.

Queste due terrazze, chiaramente separate tra loro, sono moderne e gradevoli. La pietra arenaria portoghese si armonizza con il klinker delle murature laterali nonché con il legno delle spalliere e dei contenitori di piante. Un richiamo visivo marcato è rappresentato dal canale con piante sistemato con ciottoli neri.

Splay Space

Landscape architecture: Hugh Ryan
Project location: Dublin, Ireland
www.hughryan.ie
Photos: Hugh Ryan

Ipe Wood Floor

Landscape architecture: Jacques Casalini
Project location: Marseille, France
www.createurjardin.ift.fr
Photos: Haike Falkenberg

Twin Garden (made of concrete)

Landscape architecture: Evelin Kohler-Ruh
Project location: Ehrenkirchen, Germany
Photos: Firma Braun – Ideen aus Stein

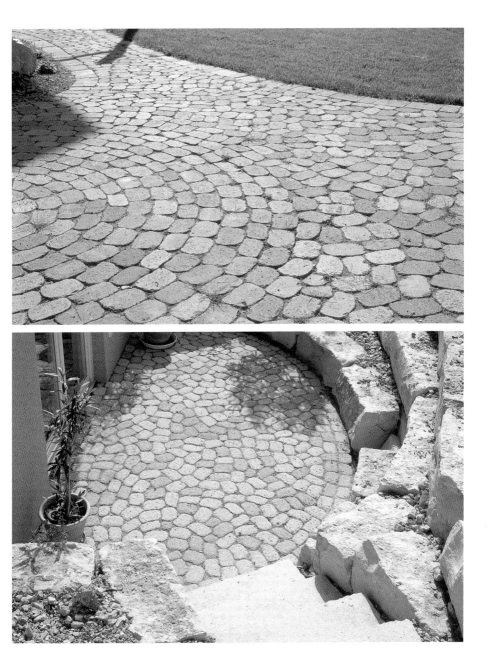

PRACTICAL AND NECESSARY . Twin Garden (made of concrete)

Three Fences

Landscape architecture: Cédric Pain
Project location: La Baule-Escoublac, France
www.painpaysage.com
Photos: Dominique Narbeburu

Large window doors have been installed into this house within a refurbishment phase, which required effective blinds to the street. Two undulating fences of iroko wood or schist steles limit the small garden and the glass door, which is decorated with bamboo images, can be opened as pleased.

Im Rahmen der Modernisierung wurden in das Haus große Fenstertüren eingebaut, die einen effektiven Sichtschutz zur Straße hin erforderten. Zwei wellenförmige Zäune aus Iroko-Holz beziehungsweise Schieferstelen begrenzen den kleinen Garten, und das mit Bambusabbildungen verzierte Glastor kann nach Wunsch geöffnet werden.

Dans le cadre d'une mesure de modernisation, des grandes portes fenêtres ont été ajoutées ; celles-ci, toutefois, devaient être protégées des regards indiscrets venant de la rue. Deux clôtures de jardin de forme ondulée en bois d'iroko et des stèles d'ardoise limitent le petit jardin et la porte de verre décorée par des bambous stylisés peut être ouverte quand on le désire.

A raíz de la última modernización de la casa se instalaron grandes puertas ventanas que requerían una protección muy efectiva contra la vista desde la calle. Dos vallas en forma de onda de madera Iroko y separadores de tiza, respectivamente limitan el pequeño jardín. El portal de cristal decorado con reproducciones de bambú se puede abrir a voluntad del propietario.

Nell'ambito della ristrutturazione dell'edificio sono state inserite grandi porte finestre che hanno richiesto un'effettiva protezione dalla visuale fino alla strada. Due recinzioni ondulate in iroko o stele in ardesia fanno da confine del piccolo giardino e la porta in vetro decorata con figure in bambù può, volendo, essere aperta.

Split Level

Landscape architecture: Hugh Ryan
Project location: Dublin, Ireland
www.hughryan.ie
Photos: Hugh Ryan

An extension to the residential building required the garden to be redesigned. The rear property has been separated horizontally by raising up one area. The vertical separation was implemented by the erection of a waist-high wall and the planting of bamboo. The wall was painted in the same friendly orange as the garden fence.

Ein Anbau an das Wohnhaus erforderte die Umgestaltung des Gartens. Das hintere Grundstück wurde horizontal geteilt, indem ein Bereich aufgeschüttet wurde, und vertikal durch die Errichtung einer hüfthohen Mauer und der Pflanzung von Bambus. Die Mauer wurde in demselben freundlichen Orangeton gestrichen wie der Gartenzaun.

En raison d'un agrandissement de la maison d'habitation, il fut nécessaire de modifier le jardin. Le terrain situé à l'arrière a été partagé horizontalement en remblayant une partie et, verticalement, en construisant un mur à la hauteur de la taille et en plantant des bambous. Le mur a été peint dans la même couleur orange chaude que la clôture du jardin.

La construcción de un anexo a la casa obligó a reestructurar el jardín. El terreno de la parte trasera se dividió horizontalmente al rellenar de tierra una de las partes y verticalmente mediante la construcción de un muro separador de media altura y posterior plantación de bambú. El muro fue luego pintado en la misma tonalidad alegre del naranja con el que se pintó la verja del jardín.

L'aggiunta di un fabbricato ad un edificio adibito ad abitazione ha richiesto la ristrutturazione del giardino. Il terreno posteriore è stato suddiviso orizzontalmente, innalzando un'area e, in senso verticale, erigendo un muro coi fianchi alti e piantando bambù. Il muro è stato verniciato con la stessa piacevole tonalità arancione della recinzione del giardino.

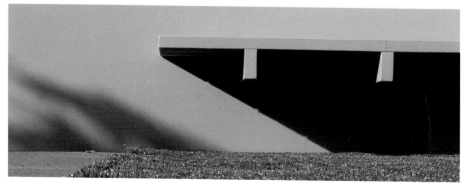

PRACTICAL AND NECE

Wooden Deck with Sea View

Landscape architecture: Jacques Casalini
Project location: Marseille, France
www.createurjardin.ift.fr
Photos: Haike Falkenberg

The round dining table is on the second of three levels of this wood-terraced garden. A customized sun canvas provides protection from the intensive midday sun and grants insights to the architecture. The fixtures have been adapted to the garden's motto, which is reminiscent of the deck of a ship.

Der runde Esstisch steht auf der mittleren der drei Ebenen dieses mit Holz terrassierten Gartens. Ein maßgefertigtes Sonnensegel schützt vor der intensiven Mittagssonne und lässt Durchblicke auf die Architektur zu. Die Halterungen wurden auf das Motto des Gartens, der an ein Schiffsdeck erinnert, abgestimmt.

Une table à manger ronde est au centre des trois niveaux de ce jardin aménagé en terrasses de bois. Une voile d'ombre sur mesures protège du soleil intense de midi et laisse un aperçu sur l'architecture. Les supports ont été dessinés selon le motif du jardin : le pont d'un navire.

La mesa redonda para comer se encuentra situada en el central de los tres niveles de madera a modo de terrazas que se han creado en este jardín. Una lona parasol fabricada a medida protege contra el rabioso sol del mediodía y permite alguna que otra vista de la arquitectura. Es de suponer que las sujeciones se adaptaron al lema de este jardín que nos recuerda un poco a la cubierta de un barco.

Il tavolo circolare si trova sul livello medio di tre livelli di questo giardino terrazzato con legno. Una tenda da sole realizzata su misura protegge dal forte sole del mezzogiorno e lascia penetrare sguardi sull'architettura dell'edificio. I supporti sono stati adattati allo stemma del giardino che ricorda il ponte di una nave.

Beccaria

Landscape architecture: sabz
Project location: Paris, France
www.sabz.fr
Photos: Nathalie Pasquel

An individual concept consisting of pergola and two sun canvases on top of each other provides for coziness and sun protection on this roof terrace. Safety aspects such as wind protection and blinds are fulfilled from a white balustrade, dark green espaliers and a bamboo wall.

Eine individuelle Konzeption aus Pergola und zwei übereinander gelegten Sonnensegeln sorgt auf dieser Dachterrasse für Behaglichkeit und Sonnenschutz. Sicherheitsaspekte sowie Wind- und Sichtschutz werden von einer weißen Balustrade, dunkelgrünen Spalieren sowie einer Bambuswand wahrgenommen.

Une conception individuelle associant une pergola et deux voiles d'ombre superposées protège cette terrasse toit du soleil et lui confère une ambiance subtile. La protection contre la brise et les regards indiscrets de même que la sécurité est assurée par une balustrade blanche, des espaliers vert sombre et un mur de bambous.

Una concepción muy individual compuesta por una pérgola y dos lonas tapa sol superpuestas, aseguran el confort y la protección solar en este ático. Los aspectos de seguridad y de protección contra el viento y las vistas no deseadas se han encargado a una balaustrada en blanco, a una serie de celosías en verde oscuro y una pared de bambú.

Un concetto individuale di pergola e di due tende da sole poste l'una sopra l'altra fa in modo che su questa terrazza per tetto vi sia agio e protezione dal sole. Gli aspetti relativi alla sicurezza, quali ad esempio protezione dal vento e dagli sguardi di estranei vengono garantiti da una balaustra bianca, da spalliere verde scuro nonché da una parete di bambù.

Private Desert Retreat

Landscape architecture: Vladimir Djurovic Landscape Architecture
Project location: Yaafur, Syria
www.vladimirdjurovic.com
Photos: Geraldine Bruneel

Garden House Delphin

Landscape architecture: Walter Naegeli, Gudrun Sack
Project location: Zurich, Switzerland
www.naegeliarchitekten.de
Photos: Walter Naegeli

Sun Sails

Landscape architecture: Artesun
Project location: Marseille, France
www.artesun.com
Photos: sunsquare and artesun

Regent's Park Garden

Landscape architecture: Amir Schlezinger
Project location: North London, UK
www.mylandscapes.co.uk
Photos: Amir Schlezinger

In the evening, this small garden experiences a magical metamorphosis. The transitions of the colors, which have been chosen for the walls and water basins, are blurring and the contrasts with the light wood and floor are coming forward. The warm lighting underneath the bench forms a comforting unit with the fireplace in the living space.

In der Abendstimmung erfährt dieser kleine Garten eine zauberhafte Verwandlung. Die Übergänge der für die Wände und das Wasserbecken gewählten Farben verschwimmen und die Kontraste mit dem hellen Holz und Boden treten hervor. Die warme Beleuchtung unter der Bank bildet eine beruhigende Einheit mit dem Kamin im Wohnraum.

Dans l'ambiance du soir ce petit jardin connaît une métamorphose, quasi, un enchantement. Les transitions des couleurs choisies pour les murs et les bassins d'eau disparaissent et les contrastes entre le bois clair et le sol passent au premier plan. L'éclairage chaud sous le banc crée une unité de forme apaisante avec la cheminée placée dans le salon.

Iluminado por la tenue luz del atardecer este pequeño jardín empieza a experimentar un cambio como si de una metamorfosis mágica se tratara. Las transiciones de los colores elegidos para decorar las paredes y la piscina de agua, empiezan a difumarse al tiempo que se acentúan los contrastes entre la madera clara y el suelo. La cálida iluminación debajo del banco forma una unidad tranquilizadora junto con la chimenea dentro del salón.

Nell'atmosfera serale, in questo piccolo giardino ha luogo un'incantevole trasformazione. Le sfumature dei colori scelti per le pareti e per i bacini d'acqua si confondono e i contrasti con il legno chiaro ed il pavimento si fanno marcati. La calda illuminazione sotto la panchina costituisce un'unità tranquillizzante con il camino posto nell'area ad uso abitativo.

Casa Natura

Landscape architecture: Patrizia Pozzi with Blackout (light project) and Fantini Mosaici (mosaic and marble)
Project location: Milan, Italy
www.patriziapozzi.it
Photos: Dario Fusaro

No matter if day or night—this garden is an artful orchestration in green and white, which is a feast for the eye in any weather. Spotlights in the ground and the support walls draw uniform reflections into the dark leaves of the hedge and highlight individual trees and the quadratic wall at the end of the garden.

Ob bei Tag oder bei Nacht, dieser Garten ist eine Inszenierung in Grün und Weiß, die bei jeder Witterung ein Augenschmaus ist. Im Boden und in den Stützmauern eingelassene Strahler zeichnen gleichmäßige Reflexe ins dunkle Heckenlaub und beleuchten einzelne Bäume sowie die quadratische Wand am Ende des Gartens.

Que ce soit le jour ou la nuit, ce jardin est une mise en scène en vert et blanc qui constitue un délice visuel par tous les temps. Des réflecteurs intégrés au sol et aux murs de soutien soulignent les mouvements réguliers et la réflexion des feuillages de la haie, éclairent et détachent ainsi certains arbres ainsi que le mur carré à l'extrémité du jardin.

Tanto de día como de noche, este jardín es una puesta en escena en blanco y verde que resulta un placer para la vista con total independencia del tiempo que hace o deja de hacer. Los focos instalados en el suelo y en los muros de contención pintan unos reflejos uniformes sobre el follaje oscuro de los setos a la vez que resaltan árboles individuales con una iluminación directa e iluminan el muro cuadrado en el fondo del jardín.

Di giorno o di notte, questo giardino rappresenta una messa in scena in verde e in bianco che con ogni tempo atmosferico rappresenta un piacere per gli occhi. Riflettori inseriti nel pavimento e nelle murature di sostegno disegnano riflessi uniformi nel fogliame di cespuglio scuro ed illuminano singoli alberi nonché la parete quadrata alla fine del giardino.

South Melbourne Residence

Landscape architecture: Jenny Smith Gardens; Lighting: Light on Landscape PTY LTD
Project location: Melbourne, Australia
www.jsg.net.au, www.lightonlandscape.com.au
Photos: Peter Clarke, Latitude Group

Magic, fun and drama arise at the push of a button: the LEDs that are located under the overhanging stone table are changing their color from blue to green and magenta. The garden receives more depths thanks to the cactuses being spotlighted and the cyan tiles of the swimming-pool are temptingly shining in the white light.

Magie, Spaß und Dramatik entstehen auf Knopfdruck: die unter dem auskragenden Steintisch platzierten LED-Leuchten verändern ihre Farbe von Blau zu Grün bis Magentarot. Durch das Anstrahlen der Kakteen erhält der Garten mehr Tiefe, und die zyanblauen Kacheln des Schwimmbeckens schimmern verführerisch im weißen Licht.

La magie, le jeu, l'enchantement ou le drame prennent forme en appuyant sur un bouton : la couleur de diodes luminescentes placées sous la table de pierre en saillie peut passer du bleu et du vert au rouge magenta. L'illumination des cactées prête une profondeur accrue au jardin tandis que les carreaux bleus de cyan de la piscine reluisent dans une lumière blanche séduisante.

Magia, diversión y drama ocurren a la vez con sólo pulsar un botón: las potentes luces de LEDs ocultadas debajo del saliente de la mesa de piedra cambian su color de azul a verde y hasta el rojo magenta. Al caer la luz de los potentes focos sobre los cactus, el jardín empieza a ganar en profundidad, mientras que las baldosas de azul cian de la piscina parecen encenderse y se difuman de forma tentadora en la blanca luz.

Magia, divertimento e dramma nascono premendo un tasto: le lampade a LED poste sotto il tavolo in pietra sporgente cambiano il loro colore da blu a verde a rosso magenta. Con l'irraggiamento delle piante cactacee il giardino riceve maggiore profondità, le piastrelle di maiolica in blu cian della piscina brillano in modo seducente di luce bianca.

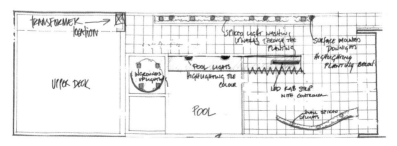

South Yarra Residence

Landscape architecture: Paul Bangay; Lighting: Light on Landscape PTY LTD
Project location: Melbourne, Australia
www.paulbangay.com, www.lightonlandscape.com.au
Photos: Peter Clarke, Latitude Group

The designers and owners of this upbeat terrace garden really proved courageous. The garden's originality only comes to its own when the lights are turned on. The light design is based on vertically aligned spotlights and a small lantern on the table; the red LED lights in the swimming-pool provide for contrasts.

Mut bewiesen haben die Designer und Eigentümer dieses peppigen Terrassengartens, dessen Originalität erst durch seine Beleuchtung richtig zur Geltung kommt. Der Beleuchtungsentwurf basiert auf vertikal ausgerichteten Strahlern und einer kleinen Laterne auf dem Tisch; die roten LED-Lichter im Schwimmbad sorgen für Kontrast.

Les propriétaires et les designers de ce jardin en terrasse pimpant ont fait preuve de courage : son originalité n'est vraiment mise en relief que par son éclairage. La conception de l'éclairage est basée sur des projecteurs dirigés à la verticale ainsi que sur une petite lanterne placée sur la table ; les diodes luminescentes rouges dans la piscines font naître le contraste.

Desde luego demostraron valor los propietarios de este estrambótico jardín cuya originalidad no se aprecia del todo hasta que alguien enciende la iluminación. El concepto de la iluminación está basado en unos focos dispuestos y orientados verticalmente y una pequeña linterna ubicada en medio de la superficie de la mesa. Las rojas luces de LEDs de la piscina se encargan luego de crear los necesarios contrastes.

I progettisti e i proprietari di questo vivace giardino per terrazza hanno dimostrato di avere coraggio. La sua originalità assume un vero valore solamente grazie alla sua illuminazione. Il progetto di illuminazione si basa su riflettori allineati verticalmente e su una piccola lanterna posta sul tavolo, le luci a LED rosse nella piscina forniscono il contrasto.

Bassil Mountain Escape

Landscape architecture: Vladimir Djurovic Landscape Architecture
Project location: Faqra, Lebanon
www.vladimirdjurovic.com
Photos: Geraldine Bruneel

Lightswing

Design: Lervik design
www.lervik.se
Manufacturer: Lervik design
Photos: Helene PE

This light swing lights up a whole garden in a most beautiful way. The creative Swedish design company incorporated this fiber optic into a see-through plastic corpus. The swing movements create a spectacular light show that does not only highly pleasure kids.

Einen ganzen Garten kann diese Leuchtschaukel auf bezaubernde Weise erhellen. Die kreative schwedische Designfirma baute Fiberoptik in einen durchsichtigen Plastikkörper ein. Durch die Schaukelbewegung entsteht ein magisches Lichtspiel, das nicht nur Kindern großes Vergnügen bereitet.

Cette balançoire lumineuse peut éclairer tout un jardin et le plonger dans l'enchantement. La firme de design suédoise créative a disposé des fibres optiques dans un corps de plastique transparent. Les mouvements de la balançoire font naître des jeux de lumière qui ne fascinent pas seulement les enfants.

Este columpio luminoso es capaz de iluminar de forma mágica a todo un jardín. La creativa firma sueca de diseños, tuvo la idea de introducir fibra óptica en el interior de un cuerpo plástico transparente. A causa del movimiento del columpio se produce un juego mágico de luces que sin duda y no tan sólo a los pequeños produce una sensación de gran fascinación.

Questa altalena luminosa può rischiarare un intero giardino in modo affascinante. La creativa ditta svedese di progettazione ha costruito una fibra ottica in un corpo di plastica trasparente. Con il movimento dell'altalena si crea un magico gioco di luci che dà un grande divertimento non solamente ai bambini.

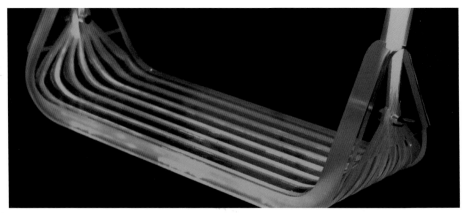

Bloom

Design: Rob Slewe, Rebecca Potger
Manufacturer: Bloom Holland BV
www.bloomholland.nl
Photos: courtesy Bloom

Piek

Design: Sebastian David Büscher
Manufacturer: IP44
www.ip44.de
Photos: Dieter Zobel

Edge

Manufacturer: IP44
www.ip44.de
Photos: Dieter Zobel

Sky

Design: Alfredo Häberli
Manufacturer: Luceplan
www.luceplan.com
Photos: courtesy Luceplan

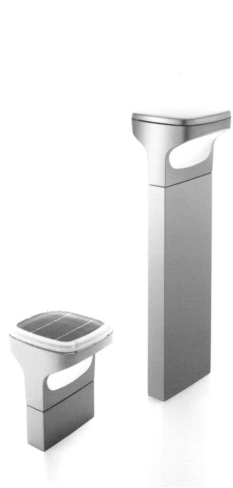

Pod Lens

Design: Ross Lovegrove
Manufacturer: Luceplan
www.luceplan.com
Photos: courtesy Luceplan

Amax

Design: Charles Williams
Manufacturer: FontanaArte
www.fontanaarte.it
Photos: Leo Torri

Flora

Design: Future Systems
Manufacturer: FontanaArte
www.fontanaarte.it
Photos: Vittoria Vergaglia

Oil Lamps

Design: Pernille Vea
Manufacturer: Menu
www.menuas.com
Photos: courtesy Menu

Oxygène

Design: Oxygène
Manufacturer: Oxygène
www.oxygene-lumiere.com, www.oxygene-design.com
Photos: courtesy Oxygène

As a matter of course, wall papers, pictures and other decoration objects for the house deserve closer attention. This devotion should also be stretched out to the décor of the garden. The choice of plants with their leafage, their growth properties and the blossoms' colors and shapes play an important role here as well, of course. However, in the end, the decision for ground level, elevated or lowered beds with or without bordering, planting pots and containers are also important for the visual effect.

Es ist selbstverständlich, Tapeten, Bildern und anderen Dekorationsobjekten des Hauses Aufmerksamkeit zu widmen. Dies lässt sich auch auf die Ausstattung des Gartens übertragen. Natürlich spielt die Auswahl der Pflanzen mit ihrem Blattwerk, ihren Wachstumseigenschaften, Blütenfarben und -formen eine zentrale Rolle. Am Ende ist aber auch die Entscheidung für ebenerdige, erhöhte oder abgesenkte Beete mit oder ohne Einfassung, Pflanztöpfe und -container ausschlaggebend für die optische Wirkung.

Les tapisseries, les tableaux et les autres objets destinés à la décoration de l'habitat doivent faire, bien sûr, l'objet d'une attention toute particulière. Il en sera de même pour la décoration du jardin. Le choix des plantes qui s'orientera sur leur feuillage, les particularités de leur croissance, les couleurs et les formes de leurs fleurs jouera naturellement un rôle de premier plan. Mais en définitive, les effets optiques seront aussi déterminés par la disposition spatiales des parterres qui, certes, peuvent être au même niveau que le terrain ou, au contraire, surélevés ou abaissés et pour lesquels on choisira, ou non, une bordure. Dans cet esprit, l'utilisation de pots, des bacs ou des conteneurs ne manquera pas non plus d'importance.

Es totalmente normal dedicar su atención al papel pintado, a los cuadros de la pared y a los restantes objetos decorativos de la casa. Estas premisas se pueden trasladar una a una al jardín. Por supuesto el protagonismo recae en la sabia selección de las plantas, con su follaje, sus características de crecimiento y el color y las formas de sus flores, de igual modo, al final influye en el efecto visual la decisión en lo que respecta a su perfecta colocación a ras del suelo, elevado o enterrado, con y sin borde, maceta o contenedor.

È naturale che si debba prestare attenzione a tappezzerie, quadri e ad altre decorazioni della casa. Ciò si può trasmettere anche all'equipaggiamento del giardino. Come è ovvio, la scelta delle piante con la forma delle foglie, le loro caratteristiche di crescita, i colori e le forme dei fiori svolge un ruolo centrale. Alla fine tuttavia, decisiva per l'effetto ottico è decidere la realizzazione di aiuole a livello del suolo, elevate o abbassate, con o senza recinto, vasi e contenitori per piante.

Battersea Terrace

Landscape architecture: Amir Schlezinger
Project location: South London, UK
www.mylandscapes.co.uk
Photos: Amir Schlezinger

The roof terrace of this penthouse in London is designed for living. The planting is therefore limited to a long, elevated bed that provides backing for the wooden bench as well as to a tailored, slender bowl. It is a beautiful eye-catcher from the interior as well.

Auf der Dachterrasse dieses Londoner Penthouses soll vor allem gelebt werden. Die Bepflanzung beschränkt sich daher auf ein langes, hochgelegenes Beet, das der Holzbank Rückendeckung bietet, sowie auf eine maßgefertigte schmale Schale. Sie ist auch vom Innenraum betrachtet ein hübscher Blickfang.

Le toit-terrasse de ce Penthouse Londonien doit surtout offrir une place à la vie de société. Les plantes se limitent à un long parterre placé en hauteur qui s'offre comme soutien à un long banc de bois ainsi qu'une coupe étroite fabriquée sur mesure. Vue de l'intérieur elle constitue aussi un point de mire esthétique.

En la terraza de este Penthouse londinense se pretende, sobre todo, vivir. Es al menos una de las razones por la cual el enfoque de jardín se limita a un solo y alargado arriate en un plano superior que sirve de respaldo al banco de madera y a una especie de maceta estrecha fabricada a medida que es también lo que atrae a la vista mirando desde el interior.

Sulla terrazza per tetto di questo attico londinese si deve anzitutto vivere. La piantumazione si limita quindi ad un'aiuola lunga e posta in alto, la quale offre alla panca in legno una copertura per le spalle nonché ad una stretta conchiglia realizzata su misura. Vista dall'interno dell'edificio essa appare particolarmente carina.

Flower Pots, Planters and Containers

Design: Amir Schlezinger
Manufacturer: MyLandscapes
www.mylandscapes.co.uk
Photos: Amir Schlezinger

DECORATION . Flower Pots, Planters and Containers   193

Splay Space

Landscape architecture: Hugh Ryan
Project location: Dublin, Ireland
www.hughryan.ie
Photos: Hugh Ryan

This design is based on a sophisticated system of eleven different levels. Central points of this design are two water ponds that act as mirrors to the sky. The upper pond is raised about 45 centimeters (18 inches) over the wooden deck. From here, water flows to the lower pond via a stone lip.

Dieser Entwurf basiert auf einem ausgeklügelten System elf verschiedener Ebenen. Zentraler Punkt sind dabei die beiden den Himmel spiegelnden Wasserflächen. Das obere Becken erhebt sich 45 Zentimeter über der Holzterrasse. Von hier fließt das Wasser über einen steinernen Ausgießer in das untere Becken.

Cette conception est fondée sur un système ingénieux réunissant onze plans différents. Le point central est formé par les deux surfaces d'eau qui reflètent le ciel. Le bassin supérieur domine la terrasse en bois de 45 centimètres. De là, l'eau coule dans le bassin inférieur par un larmier en pierre.

Este boceto se basa en un sistema muy elaborado de once niveles distintos siendo el punto central las dos superficies de agua que reflejan el cielo. El estanque superior se eleva unos 45 centimetros por encima de la terraza de madera. Desde aquí el agua pasa al estanque inferior a través de un vertedero de piedra.

Questa bozza si fonda su un sistema sofisticato rappresentato da undici diversi livelli. Il punto centrale è rappresentato da due distese d'acqua che si riflettono nel cielo. La vasca superiore si eleva per 45 centimetri sopra la terrazza di legno. Da qui l'acqua fluisce nella vasca inferiore attraverso un beccuccio versatore in pietra.

Large Family Garden

Landscape architecture: Charlotte Rowe Garden Design
Project location: London, UK
www.charlotterowe.com
Photos: Marianne Majerus

A narrow 'letter box' style spout of water falls from an apron wall into the main infinity-edge pool, making a lovely splashing sound on the terrace and into the house. The water then flows over the entire width of the pool into a narrow rill filled with pebbles and out into the lawn. The pool can be crossed by stepping stones made of poured concrete.

Ein schmaler Schlitz in der weißen Wand füllt das Becken und bereichert den Garten um das angenehme Geräusch plätschernden Wassers. Zur Rasenfläche hin fließt das Wasser über die gesamte Beckenbreite in eine mit Kies gefüllte Rinne, die sich an einer Seite wie ein Balken in den Rasen schiebt. Sehr originell sind auch die Trittstufen im Becken.

Une fente étroite pratiquée dans le mur blanc remplit le bassin et enrichit le jardin du clapotement agréable de l'eau. L'eau se dirige vers le gazon sur toute la largeur du bassin dans une gouttière remplie de gravier qui, d'un côté s'enfonce dans le gazon à l'instar d'une poutre. Les marches du bassin font aussi preuve de la plus grande originalité.

Una estrecha ranura en la pared blanca llena el estanque y enriquece al jardín al añadir el agradable sonido del murmullo del agua al caer. En dirección hacia la manta verde del césped, el agua rebosa en toda la anchura el borde del estanque y se vierte en un canalón lleno de grava que por uno de los lados avanza en el césped como si de una viga de madera se tratara. Muy originales son también los peldaños del estanque.

Una stretta fessura nella parete bianca riempie la vasca ed arricchisce il giardino del piacevole rumore di acqua gorgogliante. Fino alla superficie del prato l'acqua fluisce lungo l'intera ampiezza della vasca fino a giungere in un canale riempito di ghiaia che si estende su un lato come una trave nell'erba. Sono molto originali anche gli scalini posto nella vasca.

Zinc Fountains

Design: Atelier du Zinc
Manufacturer: Atelier du Zinc
www.atelierzinc.com
Photos: Atelier du Zinc

The "Atelier du Zinc" knows how to turn robust metal into fancy items such as state-of-the-art planters, frisky bar counters, washing basins and sinks according to historic models or multiple fountains. Various techniques provide for the permanent color of the tailor-made pieces.

Die Firma Atelier du Zinc weiß aus dem widerstandsfähigen Metall originelle Gegenstände zu fertigen, beispielsweise moderne Pflanzkübel, verspielte Bartheken, Wasch- und Spülbecken nach historischen Vorbildern oder mannigfaltige Brunnen. Verschiedene Techniken erlauben die dauerhafte Färbung der maßgefertigten Stücke.

La maison « Atelier du zinc » sait transformer un matériau résistant en objets originaux tels que de modernes cubes pour plantes, des bars enjoués, des lavabos et des éviers selon des modèles historiques ou historisants ainsi que des fontaines de toutes sortes. Différentes techniques permettent de donner une couleur durable à ces pièces faites sur mesures.

La firma Atelier du Zinc sabe como nadie fabricar objetos muy originales con el resistente material que es el cinc, como por ejemplo macetas para plantas de mucha actualidad, barras de bar muy juguetonas, pilas y cubetas réplicas de originales históricos o fuentes de todo tipo. Diferentes técnicas de fabricación permiten la coloración permanente y duradera de las piezas fabricadas a medida.

La ditta Atelier du Zinc sa realizzare originali oggetti partendo dal metallo resistente, ad esempio moderni vasi per piante, frivole teche per bar, lavandini e lavelli secondo modelli storici o fontane multiformi. Diverse tecniche permettono la colorazione durevole dei pezzi prodotti su misura.

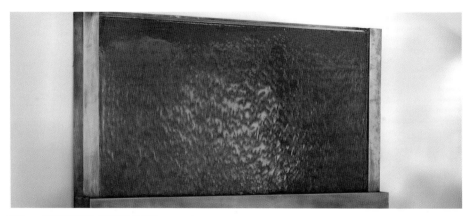

Timeless Elegance

Landscape architecture: Charlotte Rowe Garden Design
Project location: Chiswick, London, UK
www.charlotterowe.com
Photos: Charlotte Rowe

"Timeless Elegance"—the name says it all here. The choice of plants, the design in terms of color, the decoration and even the water features—are all elegant and timeless. After dark, an underwater spotlight lights up the small water rill in this sympathetically designed garden in London.

„Timeless Elegance" – hier ist der Name Programm. Die Wahl der Pflanzen, die farbliche Gestaltung, die Dekoration bis hin zum Brunnen, in diesem Gärtchen ist alles elegant und zeitlos. Bei Dunkelheit rückt ein Unterwasserstrahler den kleinen Ausguss in den Mittelpunkt dieses liebevoll gestalteten Gartens in London.

« Timeless Elegance » – Ici le nom est tout un programme. Le choix des plantes, la composition des couleurs, la décoration et jusqu'aux fontaines, tout dans ce jardin est élégant et classique. La nuit, un spot placé sous l'eau met cette fontaine au centre de ce jardin londonien aménagé avec amour.

"Timeless Elegance"– En este caso el nombre de por sí es un programa. La elección de las plantas, la concepción de los colores, la decoración hasta el pozo, todo en este jardín es elegante y atemporal. Al caer la noche un foco subacuático se encarga de centrar la atracción en el pequeño vertedero de este jardín de Londres realizado con tanto cariño.

"Timeless Elegance" – un nome che è tutto un programma. La scelta delle piante, l'impostazione dei colori, la decorazione fino alla fontana, in questo piccolo giardino tutto è elegante e non soggetto al tempo. Quando è buio un riflettore subacqueo fa apparire il piccolo acquaio al centro di questo giardino di Londra realizzato in modo accurato.

Sundials "Water Wall"

Design: David Harber
Manufacturer: David Harber
www.davidharbersundials.co.uk
Photos: Clive Nichols

Where there is water, there is life. But not only that—there are also motion, reflections and sounds. David Harber's designs create fascinating points of rest for the ears and the eyes. Thanks to state-of-the-art technology and finest quality material, he and his team create individual works for eternity.

Wo Wasser ist, ist Leben. Und nicht nur das, auch Bewegung, Reflexe und Geräusche. Die Kreationen David Harbers schaffen faszinierende Ruhepunkte für das Gehör und die Augen. Dank moderner Technologie und bester Materialien fertigt er mit seinem Team individuelle Werke für die Ewigkeit.

La vie est là où se trouve l'eau. Et non seulement la vie mais aussi le mouvement, les réflexions et les bruits. Les créations de David Harber créent des pôles de repos fascinants pour l'ouie et la vue. Grâce à une technologie moderne, les meilleurs matériaux et à son équipe il fabrique des objets individuels pour l'éternité.

Donde hay agua hay vida, y no sólo esto, también hay movimiento, reflejos y sonidos. Las creaciones de David Harber crean puntos de descanso fascinantes para el oído y la vista de las personas. Gracias a las últimas tecnologías y el uso de materiales de primer orden él y su equipo fabrican obras para la eternidad.

Dove c'è acqua c'è anche vita. E non solo questo, ma anche movimento, riflessi e rumori. Le creazioni di David Harber creano affascinanti punti di riposo per udito ed occhi. Grazie ad una moderna tecnologia e ai migliori materiali l'autore, insieme al suo team, realizza lavori individuali per l'eternità.

Elie Saab Residence

Landscape architecture: Vladimir Djurovic Landscape Architecture
Project location: Faqra, Lebanon
www.vladimirdjurovic.com
Photos: Geraldine Bruneel, Sketch by VDLA

A seat and a swimming-pool could hardly be designed in a more simple way. The residential blocks of stone and the water level prepare the eye for spectacular view over the wonderful desert scenery. At night, when the stony fireplaces are ignited, this place airs pure magic.

Schlichter kann man einen Sitzplatz und einen Swimmingpool kaum gestalten. Die herrschaftlichen Steinquader und der Wasserspiegel bereiten das Auge auf den Ausblick über die grandiose Wüstenlandschaft vor. Bei Nacht, wenn in den Steinbecken Feuer entzündet werden, strahlt der Platz pure Magie aus.

Il est à peine possible de concevoir un siège et une piscine aussi sobre. Les blocs de pierres nobles et la surface de l'eau préparent l'oeil à un aperçu sur un paysage désertique grandiose. La nuit, quand des feux sont allumés dans les bassins de pierre, une magie pure se dégage de cet endroit.

Sería difícil concebir un sitio donde sentarse y una piscina de más sencillez. Las majestuosas piedras y la superficie del agua preparan la vista para la grandiosa panorámica del paisaje de desierto que se ofrece a continuación. Cuando cae la noche y se encienden los fuegos entre las piedras, el sitio irradia magia en estado puro.

È difficile arredare un posto dove sedersi ed una piscina in modo più sobrio. Le eleganti pietre squadrate e lo specchio d'acqua preparano all'occhio una visione sul grandioso panorama desertico. Di notte, quando nel bacino in pietra vengono accesi i fuochi, il luogo irradia pura magia.

Charlotte Rowe's Garden

Landscape architecture: Charlotte Rowe Garden Design
Project location: London, UK
www.charlotterowe.com
Photos: Clive Nichols

It is hard to say if this garden is actually a garden—or a room without a roof. The range of inviting seating, the superb materials and the perfectly coordinated lighting could be compared with high-quality interior design. The icing on the cake is, without doubt, the stylish open fireplace.

Es ist schwer zu sagen, ob dieser Garten eigentlich noch ein Garten ist – oder ein Raum ohne Dach. Die Vielfalt der einladenden Sitzgelegenheiten, die superben Materialien und die perfekt abgestimmte Beleuchtung scheuen keinen Vergleich mit hochwertiger Innenarchitektur. Tüpfelchen auf dem i ist zweifellos der geschmackvolle Kamin.

Il est difficile de dire si ce jardin est encore un jardin où une pièce sans toit. La variété des sièges, les matériaux superbes et l'éclairage parfaitement calculé peuvent soutenir la comparaison avec une architecture intérieure de haut niveau. Le fin du fin est, sans aucun doute, la cheminée du meilleur goût.

Es difícil decidir si este jardín en el fondo sigue siendo un jardín o más bien una habitación sin techo. El gran número de ofertas para sentarse y relajarse cómodamente, los exquisitos materiales y la iluminación perfectamente equilibrada y coordinada, todo ello ya forma parte del mundo del interiorismo y puede ser perfectamente juzgado para estas premisas. Un punto y aparte se consigue sin duda con la chimenea de gusto exquisito.

È difficile dire se questo giardino sia ancora un giardino – oppure un ambiente privo di tetto. La molteplicità delle possibilità di posti a sedere a disposizione, i superbi materiali e l'illuminazione perfettamente intonata non temono confronto con l'architettura d'interni di pregio. Il puntino sulla "i" è rappresentato sicuramente dal camino pieno di gusto.

David Trubridge Ltd
Design and manufacture furniture & lighting
www.davidtrubridge.com; www.dutchdd.nl
Cicada, Whakatu Industrial Park, PO Box 15
Hastings, 4161, New Zealand
+646 / 65 00 20 4
office@davidtrubridge.com

DEDON GmbH
Outdoor Furniture
www.dedon.de
Zeppelinstraße 22
21337 Lüneburg, Germany
+49 / 4131 22 44 750
office@dedon.de

driade
aesthetic workshop, design, furniture
www.driade.com
Via Padana inferiore 12
29012 Fossadello di Caorso (PC), Italy
Sales Italy +39 / 05 23 81 86 50
com.it@driade.com
International sales +39 / 05 23 81 86 60
export@driade.com

Dwell by jo
Furniture and interior design
www.dwellbyjo.com.au
48/22 Penkivil St
Bondi, NSW 2026, Australia
+61 / 41 45 62 055
jo@dwellbyjo.com.au

Earth Designs
Garden design and build
www.earthdesigns.co.uk
The Garden Studio, 64 Buxton Road
London E17 7EJ, UK
+44 / 20 85 21 90 40
info@earthdesigns.co.uk

eo engineering
Sun sails
www.eo-engineering.de
Eschenweg 6
85599 Parsdorf, Germany
+49 / 8104 62 96 50
gerhard.esterl@eo-engineering.de

Exonido
Outdoor furniture
www.exonido.fr
265, rue de Créqui
69003 Lyon, France
+33 / 62 67 12 838
vivredehors@exonido.fr

Extremis
Furniture and objects
www.extremis.eu
Weegschede 39
8691 Gijverinkhove, Belgium
+32 / 05 82 99 72 5

Fermob
Outdoor furniture
www.fermob.com

FontanaArte
Lighting and design
www.fontanaarte.it
Alzaia Trieste 49
20094 Corsico (Milano), Italy
+39 / 02 45 12 1
info@fontanaarte.it

Gandia Blasco
Furniture, textiles
www.gandiablasco.com
C/ Musico Vert, 4
46870 Ontinyent (Valencia), Spain
+34 / 90 25 30 30 2
info@gandiablasco.com

HONEYMOON – GWA SARL
Gazebo, daybed & pergolas
www.honeymoon-world.com
282, route des Cistes
06600 Antibes, France
+33 / 49 36 19 535
europe@honeymoon-world.com

Hugh Ryan Landscape Design
Garden design and construction
www.hughryan.ie
27 Fastnet Court, Marina Village
Arklow, County Wicklow, Ireland
+353 / 40 24 18 41
mail@hughryan.ie

IP44
Light design
www.ip44.de
Schmalhorst GmbH & Co. KG
Marienstraße 13
33378 Rheda-Wiedenbrück, Germany
welcome@ip44.de

JEV DERBEZ
Garden design
www.derbez.fr
www.derbez-paysage.com
RD 98
83580 Gassin, France
+33 / 49 45 61 196

Jim Fogarty Design Pty Ltd
Landscape design
www.jimfogartydesign.com.au
2 Illowa Street
Malvern East, Victoria 3145, Australia
+61 / 39 81 38 55 0
jim@jimfogartydesign.com.au

KOK DIFFUSION
Outdoor and indoor furniture
www.kokmaison.com
BP 146
59433 Halluin Cedex, France
+33 / 32 02 38 976
info@kokmaison.com

La Hutte
www.lahutte-mobilier.com
20–26, quai de Queyries
33100 Bordeaux, France
+33 / 5 56 51 24 99
contact@lahutte-mobilier.com

LERVIK DESIGN
Product design
www.lervik.se
Stora Skuggans Väg 11
11542 Stockholm, Sweden
+46 / 70 54 35 535
alexander@lervik.se

Light on Landscape PTY LTD
Lighting design and lighting solutions
www.lightonlandscape.com.au
832 High Street, Armadale
Melbourne, Victoria 3143, Australia
+61 / 39 50 98 00 0
info@lightonlandscape.com.au

Living Divani
High-quality seating
www.livingdivani.com
Strada del Cavolto
22040 Anzano del Parco (CO), Italy
+39 / 03 16 30 95 4

Luceplan Spa
Light design
www.luceplan.com
Via E.T. Moneta 46
20161 Milan, Italy
+39 / 02 66 24 21
info@luceplan.com

Magis
Furniture design
www.magisdesign.it
Via Magnadola 15
31045 Motta di Livenza (TV), Italy
+39 / 04 22 86 26 00
info@magisdesign.com

MCG GmbH Artesun
Sun sails
www.artesun.com
45, allée des Ormes, BAT D, BP 1200
06254 Mougins, France
+33 / 61 43 14 006
jana.esterl@artesun.com

menu a/s
Scandinavian design
www.menuas.com
Kongevejen 2
3480 Fredensborg, Denmark
+45 / 48 40 61 00

MyLandscapes
www.mylandscapes.co.uk

NAEGELIARCHITEKTEN
Architects and designers
www.naegeliarchitekten.de
Lychenerstraße 43
10437 Berlin, Germany
+49 / 30 61 60 97 12
buero@naegeliarchitekten.de

Nils Holger Moormann GmbH
Furniture design
www.moormann.de
An der Festhalle 2
83229 Aschau im Chiemgau, Germany
+49 / 8052 90 450
info@moormann.de

Ulf Nordfjell
Landscape architect
Stockholm, Sweden
ulf.nordfjell@ramboll.se
lunab@hammarbysjostad.se

Olivebay
Garden design and construction
www.olivebay.co.uk
103 Victoria Road
Barnet, Herts EN4 9PE, UK
+44 / 20 82 75 78 78
gardens@olivebay.co.uk

Oxygène
Furniture and lighting
www.oxygene-lumiere.com
www.oxygene-design.com
6, rue du Rialet
83310 Cogolin, France
+33 / 87 54 67 862
info@oxygene-lumiere.com

SARL PAIN CONCEPT DESIGN PAYSAGE
Landscape architecture
www.painpaysage.com
23, rue de la Pigeonnière
44740 Batz sur Mer, France
+33 / 24 02 39 498
painpaysage@wanadoo.fr

Patrizia Pozzi
Landscape architecture
www.patriziapozzi.it
Corso Venezia 23
20121 Milan, Italy
+39 / 02 76 00 39 12
landscape@patriziapozzi.it

Jürgen Ruh
Garden design
Insel 14
79238 Ehrenkirchen, Germany
+49 / 7633 98 18 18
galabau-ruh.@t-online.de

sabz
Garden design and construction,
Outdoor and indoor furniture, lighting and
accessories retailer, on-line sales
www.sabz.fr
22, rue Rottembourg
75012 Paris, France
+33 / 14 02 13 005
info@sabz.fr

SALA Phuket Resort and Spa
www.salaphuket.com
333 M. 3 Mai Khao, Thalang
Phuket 83110, Thailand
+66 / 76 33 88 88
info@salaphuket.com

Six Senses Resorts & Spas
www.sixsenses.com
19/F Two Pacific Place Building,
142 Sukhumvit Road, Klongtoey,
Bangkok 10110, Thailand
+66 / 26 31 97 77
mail@sixsenses.com

Slomp & Busarello Architects
Architecture, urbanism, landscape and design
www.slompbusarello.com.br
Av. Cândido de Abreu, 526, CJ1510A
Curitiba, 81130-000, Brazil
+55 / 41 32 53 13 34
projetos@slompbusarello.com.br

smarin
Design company
www.smarin.net
32, avenue Henri Dunant, Impasse Laurenti
06100 Nice, France
+33 / 49 35 28 926
m.jessica@smarin.net

Vladimir Djurovic Landscape Architecture
Landscape architecture
www.vladimirdjurovic.com
Villa Rizk
Broumana, Lebanon
+961 / 4 86 24 44 / 555
info@vladimirdjurovic.com

YES-ARCHITECTURE
Architectural services
www.yes-architecture.com
Griesgasse 10
8020 Graz, Austria
+43 / 316 76 48 91
wicher@yes-architecture.com

Other titles by teNeues

ISBN 978-3-8327-9228-2

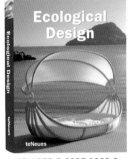

ISBN 978-3-8327-9229-9

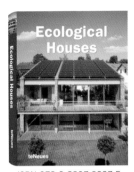

ISBN 978-3-8327-9227-5

Size: **15 x 19 cm**, 6 x 7½ in., 224 pp., **Flexicover**, c. 200 color photographs,
Text: English / German / French / Spanish / Italian

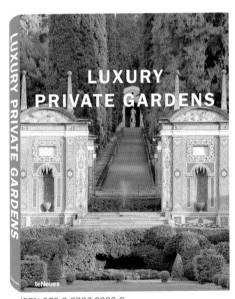

ISBN 978-3-8327-9226-8

Size: **25.6 x 32.6 cm**, 10 x 12⅞ in., 220 pp., **Hardcover with jacket**,
Text: English / German / French / Spanish / Italian

www.teneues.com

Other titles by teNeues

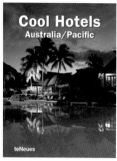

ISBN 978-3-8327-9309-8

ISBN 978-3-8327-9274-9

ISBN 978-3-8327-9237-4

ISBN 978-3-8327-9247-3

ISBN 978-3-8327-9234-3

ISBN 978-3-8327-9308-1

ISBN 978-3-8327-9243-5

ISBN 978-3-8327-9230-5

ISBN 978-3-8327-9248-0

Size: **15 x 19 cm**, 6 x 7½ in., 224 pp., **Flexicover**, c. 200 color photographs,
Text: English / German / French / Spanish / Italian
www.teneues.com